GOSPEL
IN
SHOES

✳✳✳

"How beautiful upon the mountains
are the feet of those who bring good
news, who proclaim peace, who bring
good tidings, who proclaim salvation..."
Isaiah 52:7 (NIV)

Cover by: Ashley Wickwire Sikora
Design and page composition by: Bruce Wickwire
Pen Line drawings by my sister
Pauline Wickwire Whitson,
for
the book "Pioneer Days of the Advent Movement"
by W. A. Spicer

Library of Congress Cataloging-in-Publication Data
International Standard Serial Number: 0-9707651-1-8
ISBN: 9780970765116

Printed in the United States of America by
Review and Herald Graphics

Texts quoted in this book are from the King James Version of the Bible.
Copyright © 1984, 1977 by Thomas Nelson, Inc. All rights reserved

To order additional copies of *Gospel in Shoes* by Bruce M. Wickwire, Sr.,
call 1-800-866-4307 or contact your Adventist Book Center.

Dedication

This book is dedicated to Literature Evangelists of the worldwide Seventh-day Adventist church, who for nearly a century and a half have left footprints around the circle of the earth. They go in any kind of weather or environment, enroll persons in Bible Correspondence courses, give Bible studies, and sell books and journals that proclaim heaven's love for mankind.

Bruce M. Wickwire, Sr.

Author of

The book, **Bold Journey**, and numerous articles
on
the publishing ministry of the
Seventh-day Adventist Church

The author assumes full responsibility for the accuracy of all facts and quotations as cited in this book.

WORLD PUBLISHING LEADERS MEET, WASHINGTON, D. C., 1976

Row Four, left to right: Walter Ruba, Kenneth Tilghman, Reinhard Rupp, Orval Driskell, D. R. L. Astleford. Row Three, left to right: W. J. Blacker, Vernon Bretsch, Ron Appenzeller, Clyde Kinder, Edouard Naenny, Ivan Benson. Row Two, left to right: Caleb Rosado, N. N. Viegas, D. K. Short, Joseph N. Hunt, Russell Thomas, W. Duncan Eva, Jon Knopper, Louis A. Ramirez. Row One, left to right: Rudi Henning, John Fowler, Bruce M. Wickwire, World Publishing Director (seated), Arthur L. White (grandson of Ellen and James White.)

Appreciation

To pioneer leaders who responded to the divine message "Begin to Print" by publishing literature portraying the character of God. To church appointed leaders who share that same faith and who during succeeding generations, with far-reaching vision encouraged and supported the prophetic ministry of literature evangelists, a ministry that fulfills a major role in playing out the great controversy and helps shape the world church.

To the thousands of laymen who today and throughout church history separated themselves from secular employment to become literature evangelists, carrying God's message to men everywhere.

Thanks to my wife Adele for her clear judgment, helpful suggestions, sympathetic approval of each chapter, and for her desktop publishing work on _Gospel in Shoes_. To grandson Mark Clemons for his computer expertise which made this book possible. To granddaughter Ashley Wickwire Sikora for her graphic art cover design.

I am deeply grateful to Dr. Ann Clark, Professor of English at Southern Adventist University for reading, editing, and offering imaginative suggestions enhancing the message in this book.

Special thanks to contributors of stories and pictures, and to those who read the manuscript.

Foreword

A considerable portion of the Seventh-day Adventist Church's claim to divine blessing, world growth, and economic strength is recorded in the history of its printing presses and tens of thousands of laymen who for more than one hundred years have personally gone door-to-door, island-to-island, spreading the message of the Three Angels of Revelation 14 to earth's inhabitants. Daily they devise methods of person-to-person contact evangelism to meet changing times, attitudes and cultures.

My Tribute to an Unknown Bookman

Ninety years have elapsed since the Holy Spirit moved upon the heart of a Seventh-day Adventist layman to leave secular employment to serve his church as a literature evangelist. He could have ignored the call. His obedience led my family into the Seventh-day Adventist Church. For forty years I followed in the publishing footsteps of this unknown evangelist. I, with thousands of others, am a grateful beneficiary of the soul-saving ministry of literature evangelism.

Divine Economics

Stories recorded in this book reveal the largely untold story of economic returns to the church in tithes, offerings, wills, legacies, annuities, and generous donations, past and present, resulting from over a century of ministry of literature evangelists. These stories cover several generations of converts, telling of sons and daughters who became pastors, evangelists, doctors, nurses, educators, mission pilots, ranchers, business men/women, medical missionaries, and denominational leaders at home and abroad. These individuals and their descendants continue to contribute millions of dollars to the church treasury.

The influence of the Spirit of Prophecy was unmistakably revealed to Seventh-day Adventist pioneers in 1848 with the commission "Begin to Print."

"A vision at the Rome, New York, camp meeting in September 1875 opened the eyes of the growing church toward the potential of literature evangelism. The 'young man of noble appearance' had often spoken to Ellen White in vision or dream. . . . His suggestion was to supplement preaching with appropriate reading matter, which would result in a '*hundred-fold return to the treasury.*'

"How was this supplemental work to be done? By literature evangelists, often called canvassers or colporteurs."[1] The ministry of literature evangelists, serving on the leading edge in church evangelism, built a world-wide economic highway upon which the church now travels.

While soul-winning remains first in importance, the economic river of tithes, offerings, wills, and legacies created by the ministry of literature evangelists should not be overlooked. The economic flow may be likened to fuel oils used in the United States of America for its 200,000,000 automobiles, thousands of commercial and private aircraft, heavy road building equipment, farm machinery, lawn mowers – a river flowing non-stop twenty-four hours each day through a tube, 18 feet in diameter, traveling four miles per hour.[2] Compare this illustration with God's economic flow into His church treasury, non-stop if uninterrupted, created by literature evangelists over more than a century.

Literature Evangelists as Ground Troops

During Desert Storm, after the desert had been baptized with fire from the sky, Commanding General Norman Schwarzkopf said, "We didn't conquer Kuwait until we sent in the ground troops." Literature evangelists may rightly be

[1] Herbert Douglass, Messenger of the Lord, section "Colporteur Ministry", p. 363.
[2] This oil flow information gleaned in conversation with a professor from Texas A & M.

considered "ground troops" of the Seventh-day Adventist Church. They personally contact more non Seventh-day Adventists, including many of North American Division's estimated million plus former Seventh-day Adventists, than does any other church worker group.

Chapter 12 of this writing, entitled "Higher Education," deals with the church's practical training for its future leaders by encouraging prospective pastors to meet people where they live, labor, and die. This provision throughout church history has strengthened the individual and the ministry of the church. No parent or government would consider sending its youth into battle armed with theory only. Field training is not only understandable, it is considered imperative before a young person is vested with authority to stand before and represent church congregations. Pastor Maywald Jesudass of Tamil Nadu, India, speaks frankly about this practical experience. "Field exposure is a great teacher; textbooks and classrooms a poor second."[3]

Literature Evangelism in Church History

To nearly every nation of the world, the first bearers of the Seventh-day Adventist message are literature evangelists. They take a brave position on the Lord's side in the great controversy between Christ and Satan. The result of their ministry is conversion growth versus biological or transfer growth.

Earliest Adventist church history reveals the effectiveness of literature ministry and shows that literature evangelists may have outnumbered church pastors. . . *"Colporteurs constitute a large percentage of active laborers of a conference, and should always be under the direction and control of the conference."* [4] Viewing the present through the past, literature evangelists have a church history, and their

[3]Adventist Review, December 14, 2000, p. 16.
[4]Palmer, E. R., "Our System of Publishing, Importance and How Maintained."

history helps explain the present.

It may rightly be assumed that to the growing church a large percentage of new converts added annually were the result of the labors of literature evangelists. To grasp the true soul-winning, economic picture, we turn Adventist history back a century and one-half to 1844, when in the earliest testimony of our brethren we see Joseph Bates as a colporteur. "He was a literature worker all his life," said W. A. Spicer, eleventh president of the General Conference.

Economically speaking it is reasonable to believe that worldwide, up to fifty percent of today's church funds may be traced to the ministerial labors of literature evangelists before and during the century recently ended, thus providing a rich economic inheritance for the church of today.

How Fortunate the Church

In the business world leaders would be quick to promote, support, and carefully nurture a plan that guarantees a hundred-fold return compared to investment. The plan has inspired tens of thousands to financially support that cause and influence their children over succeeding generations to join them in this commitment with its lifelong returns.

Since the day of the visit of a literature evangelist ninety years ago, my family, children, grandchildren, and great grandchildren have been supporting the church with sons, daughters, missionaries, tithes, and offerings as have thousands of other converts from literature evangelism.

With various electronic methods available for communication, including TV and internet, some might suggest that times have so changed that literature evangelism is no longer relevant, possible, or necessary. Today's 43,000 literature evangelists say, NOT SO! The message to the church is, *"The canvassing work should never languish. The agencies set in operation to do this work need always to be under the control of the Holy Spirit."* [5] *"As long as probation continues there will be opportunity for the canvasser to work."* [6]

Who Are They?

Literature evangelists, like pastors, elect to leave secular work to become gospel church workers. *"Both workers have light and both are to shine in their respective spheres of influence."* [7] They are not inclined to nurture themselves with earthly comforts; not when scripture declares an end to humankind. Courage does not always roar. Sometimes it is a quiet voice, which, if not heard today, will try again tomorrow. Wherever encouraged, literature evangelists provide a constant flow of non-Adventists into the church. As long as the church and its leaders trust scripture and Spirit of Prophecy counsel, this inflow of converts will continue and increase, a fact important to indigenous church growth in nations of the Western world.

The ministry of licensed and credentialed, full, part-time, and student literature evangelists includes the selling of gospel literature, praying with and for the people, enrolling individuals in Bible courses, and providing names of interested persons to local pastors and to conference personnel for follow-up "harvest" evangelism.

Fourteen to One, Ultimately a Full Church

Conversion of individuals, families, and entire churches, are often the result of the visit of one literature evangelist or the placing of just one book. "The Story of a Family" by Clark Lamberton, number nine of fourteen children,

---

[5] Letter 82, 1889, C.M. p. 104.
[6] Test. Vol 6. 478 (1900) C.M. p. 11.
[7] Letter 186, (1903).

reveals not only the divinely ordained evangelistic influence of the ministry of literature evangelism, it also clearly reveals the promise to the church of a "hundred-fold return to the treasury."

Of Henry and Katie's fourteen children, four became teachers, two farmers, two nurses, two orthodontists, a physician, a builder, a plumber and a homemaker. Today the Seventh-day Adventist offspring of Henry and Katie's fourteen children would fill a large church. They are all the fruit from the visit of a one-armed book salesman so many years ago.

As number nine of the fourteen children, I have lived halfway around the world from the United States for more than half of my life, so there are many near relatives I do not know. I hope we can all meet our one-armed brother, the book salesman, soon after the prophecies of Daniel and Revelation are fulfilled. I think it will be soon.[8]

In the Lamberton story the soul-winning ratio becomes the equivalent of an entire church. This fact comes as no surprise to those who understand church history and maintain trust in the Spirit of Prophecy. It is fulfillment of a divine promise to the church. Literature evangelism works today just as it did forty or one hundred years ago.

The Ministry of Literature Evangelists

The ministry of literature evangelists is compared by some scholars to the Biblical illustration in Ezekiel 47 of a gospel work beginning as a small rivulet and becoming a mighty river. It continues to play a vital role in the mission of the church. Literature evangelism is a golden thread woven into the fabric of the worldwide mission of the Seventh-day Adventist Church's

[8] Adventist Review, December 25, 2003, pp. 14-16.

evangelistic endeavor.

The author's publishing footsteps began when he left
the selling of earthly real estate to enter church ministry as
a literature evangelist. As I was called to various levels of
publishing department leadership, my responsibilities increased
to include establishment and coordination of publishing houses,
and strengthening and developing Adventist Book Centers. Books
could be written about each of these important phases of the
church's publishing ministry.

In *Gospel in Shoes* I have chosen to write about "The
Role of Literature Evangelists in World Evangelism" lest
any church member or church leader be unaware that God
not only ordained the canvassing ministry, but also built into
it divine economics. The ministry of literature evangelists
has shaped and extended the mission of the world church. In
their wake mission stations have been established, publishing
houses built and educational centers, clinics, and hospitals
set in motion. Their mission continues to create both an
evangelistic and economic highway at home and abroad, to
be built upon by other ministries. Their adventures, stories,
experiences, loneliness, health hazards, sacrifices, challenges
and even deaths are an eternal part of Adventism.

The Seventh-day Adventist church is witness today to
more than a century of gospel seed sowing by its thousands
of literature evangelists. Impressive evangelistic reports
testify to the positive effect of the world mission of literature
evangelists by the fact of hundreds and thousands of persons
now becoming Seventh-day Adventist church members,
particularly overseas.

Introduction

When Sound Dies, the Written Word Remains

In a letter dated September 2001, Pastor Doug Batchelor, Director/Speaker of Amazing Facts, made the following statement, printed in bold type: **"But the fact remains that one of the most powerful mediums for reaching the masses is the printed word.** The pen is still mightier than the sword".[9]

Widely read Seventh-day Adventist author Clifford Goldstein says, "Another thing about the printed word: it endures. Conversations fade . . . the printed page preserves the original words, unaltered and unfiltered by the blurriness of time. Long after the spoken word vanishes, the written word remains. That's the reason, with presses on every continent, there is probably not a moment in any day (except Sabbath) when an Adventist press isn't producing written material."[10] Eighty-six years ago Ellen White advised the church that the Press is a powerful means to move the minds and hearts of the people.[11]

Electronic Evangelism -- Including Internet

Television has introduced the instantaneous transmission of images with sound. At thirty-five years of age on a trip to Japan the author first saw this marvelous means for communicating the gospel. Four years later back in America it appeared that every house had grown a metal tree (antenna). Surely God provided TV and later internet as impressive methods for His people to include in their evangelistic arsenal. However, God, with knowledge of humanity's time from the very beginning until the sound

---

[9] Amazing Facts, September 2001, p. 1.
[10] Adventist Review, NAD Edition, June 1999.
[11] Christian Experience, p. 225. (1922), C.M., p. 148.

of the final trumpet, knew that in earth's closing moments people would be rushing madly about in a market-driven society, finding it difficult to slow down and listen. While every means for spreading the news of salvation is important, the value of personal contact becomes increasingly evident.

Many people thought that when the wonders of television came into existence it would replace the need for books, journals and newspapers. Not so. More books and journals are being produced today than in all human history. In a thirty-minute news telecast by any nation's popular news caster, after commercials, there would be only twenty minutes of news presentation. This would represent only one page of a daily newspaper.

Each chapter in this book provides insight into Adventist heritage through soul-winning adventure stories of literature evangelists and their economic role in world evangelism. The stories and the people are real.

In the following pages the reader is provided a mental picture of literature evangelists, not only selling millions of books and journals throughout the world, but also enrolling thousands of indigenous strangers in Bible Correspondence courses in their respective languages, with thousands becoming church members and lifelong supporters of the church.

CONTENTS

Chapter One

Chapter Two

Chapter Three

Chapter Four

Chapter Eight

Chapter Nine

Chapter Ten

Moment of Time -- Ships That Pass in the Night.

Chapter Eleven

Chapter Twelve

Chapter Thirteen

Chapter 1-
Ellis Island - Literature Evangelism

The flow of immigrants into the United States began in 1891. Ellis Island, called the "Gateway to the New World", built to handle five thousand immigrants daily, served as a United States Immigration Station from 1891 to 1954. People first came to America from Northern Europe, then from Southern Europe. The sight first to greet immigrants arriving in New York harbor by ocean liner was the awe-inspiring Statue of Liberty, the "Lady," a symbol of freedom. The people of France gave this "Lady" to the United States in 1884, a monument holding great significance to those who had suffered under tyranny, endeavored to defend freedom in halls of government, or contended on earth's battlefields. They were now in America, the land of opportunity!

Ellis Island,
a United States immigration station
until 1954, was called
"The Gateway to The New World."

America was a young nation with less than 140 miles of hard surfaced roads and fewer than 8,000 automobiles. At this time about sixteen million aliens were examined and passed through Ellis Island. As these immigrants fanned out across America, they staked claim to much of its rich land. Literature evangelists followed them from coast-to-coast, into the cities and across the prairies, endeavoring to contact each new family, that they might understand the message of Revelation 13 regarding America, their newfound land.

In Pursuit of Immigrants

Sixty-three years and more than 16,000,000 immigrants.

John Oskar Larson emigrated with his parents from Sweden more than one hundred years ago. When arriving in New York City they did not wish to become city dwellers, but chose the open prairie, and purchased tickets to the very end of the railway line, to settle in Iowa. Oskar and his brother later moved to Kansas, took out homestead claims, eventually found companions, and married.

In the fall of 1900 while Oskar was harvesting his corn, a stranger came to the Larson homestead. Swen Mortensen, a literature evangelist, was following immigrants across America's prairies. He joined Oskar in husking corn out in the field, all the while sharing the gospel. When night came, the entire family studied the Bible with this stranger, who was invited to spend the night in their home. Swen slept on the kitchen floor, the only available space in the sod house. It was not unusual for literature evangelists in early America to sleep in barns, haystacks or covered wagons. They were serious about winning souls for Christ.

Baptized in a Horse Tank

Literature Evangelist Swen Mortensen continued visiting the Larson family, and studied with them until they understood the doctrines of the Seventh-day Adventist Church and were firmly rooted in Bible truth. In due time Oskar and his wife decided to be baptized. Their baptismal tank was the horse trough from which a crust of ice was removed. Understandably, this could be classed among the coldest and briefest baptisms in church history. All parties were serious about salvation. Such commitment was passed on to children, grandchildren and great grandchildren.

The three daughters of Alma Hemme, Oskar Larson's daughter, served a total of one hundred years in the educational ministry of the Seventh-day Adventist church. The author is indebted to Thelma Cushman Wearner for providing this story, and is grateful to Leeta Hemme for her devoted teaching and Christian influence upon our daughters and son and many other young people who were students at Far Eastern Academy in Singapore.

Thelma Cushman Wearner

Leeta Hemme

Della Habenicht

The third daughter, Della, also a teacher, shares in this wonderful story of service to the Seventh-day Adventist Church. Imagine a century of Christian influence upon the lives of Seventh-day Adventist youth who sat at the feet of these dedicated teachers. Their work was preaching through teaching.

Other family members devoted their lives to work for the Seventh-day Adventist church: Albert in Seventh-day Adventist hospitals; Joseph a leader in his country church; Aaron pioneering the work of the church in Inter America; and Mabel becoming a nurse. Church history makes clear that Christian education is an integral part and a result of the ministry of literature evangelism.

Who can imagine the majesty and splendor of the scene, and the exhilaration when John Oskar Larson meets literature evangelist Swen Mortensen in heaven, and introduces him to the Larson family -- children, grandchildren and great grandchildren who have been faithful workers in the Seventh-day Adventist Church, the result of the ministry of one literature evangelist and just one book, accompanied by the ministry of the Holy Spirit.

While we have no record of other families literature evangelist Swen Mortensen won for Christ, this experience speaks for thousands of literature evangelists in the church's past history and for more than 43,000 literature evangelists currently telling the story of Jesus in over 258 languages and dialects. Listen: do you hear what I hear? It is the voices of these thousands of ministers of the printed page, their many languages blending into a heavenly symphony as they knock at strangers' doors or call at their gates.

Dried Apples or Fresh Bear Meat

Oskar Larson's granddaughter Thelma tells the story of relatives in the Ohio Valley going west to California. The family traveled in a covered wagon, laden with enough dried apples and other staples for the long journey. At nightfall the cache of dried apples was suspended high in a tree out of reach of bears.

One night the apples were apparently hung too low, or a very tall bear succeeded in reaching them. When it was discovered that the apples were gone, search led to a nearby stream of water where they found the bear, dead. Dried apples had swelled when the bear drank from the running stream. For the remainder of the journey the family subsisted on apple-flavored bear meat!

Far-reaching Influence of our Publications

In the miracle of feeding the multitude with a few loaves and fishes, the food was increased as it

*passed from Christ to those who accepted it. Thus it
will be in the distribution of our publications. God's
truth, as it is passed out, will multiply greatly. And
as the disciples by Christ's direction gathered up
the fragments which remained, that nothing should
be lost, so we should treasure every fragment of
literature containing the truth for this time.*[12]

For over 100 years Larson family members have been
serving and supporting the Seventh-day Adventist church
with sons, daughters, grandchildren, tithes, and offerings.

God Bless the Missionaries and the Colporteurs

During the writer's growing up years the prayers of
the church and of family members, including little children,
was "God bless the missionaries and the colporteurs."
Through the years God answers these petitions in a
marvelous way.

Just as fifty percent of Americans trace their origin to
Ellis Island, so up to fifty percent of Seventh-day Adventists
may trace their Adventist origin to the visit of a literature
evangelist long before, during or after the twentieth century.

Have You Ever Been to America?

The author went to the Orient to serve the church in
1948. At that time national government workers were still
serving under colonial powers. When I applied for a Dutch
East Indies (now Indonesia) residence permit, customs and
immigration workers, knowing that I was an American,
wanted to know more about the land from which flowed so
many Jeeps (World War II had just ended) and Parker 51
pens, popular at that time. My question was, "Have you

[12] *Review and Herald*, August 27, 1903.

ever been to America?" Their answer was never, "No." Instead they would say, "Not yet." Today the aggressive and progressive ones are here. Their presence and commitment enriches our church and our nation.

In War's Aftermath

In the aftermath of World War II, missionaries were sent to the Orient, Southern Asia, and elsewhere to locate church members and their leaders who survived the war and to bring them hope, fellowship, and assurance. Re-establishing church organization and rebuilding damaged or destroyed buildings was necessary.

Following the devastation of World War II the commission to missionaries was to prepare national leaders to assume administrative and departmental responsibility for the future, especially in the event of another war. In short years these church leadership positions were transferred to the hands of well-trained national leaders, resulting in a strong international church.

The Indigenous

We are presently organizing numerous churches in the North American Division and in other divisions of the western world for dedicated and devoted members of so-called third world countries. Their zeal inspires us. They are missionaries among us. Though accessions to the church reveal world-wide membership increase, the number of those who gave birth and strength to the church in the western world has not proportionately increased.

In nations where indigenous membership is static or declining, it is important to review church history and Spirit of Prophecy counsel regarding literature evangelism. To ensure a successful literature evangelist program, provision must include undistracted leadership and reasonable living subsidies for literature evangelists. Like the farmer, the literature evangelist tills the ground and sows gospel seed. Church history makes clear that the ministry of literature evangelists not only results in multiple thousands of souls won but also guarantees "a hundred-fold return to the church treasury."

Concern for Indigenous

From the beginning America has been a nation of immigrants. Pastor George R. Knight, professor of Church History at the Seventh-day Adventist Seminary, expresses concern regarding neglect of the indigenous.

George R. Knight

As a church we have done well in Africa, Asia and South America – the old mission fields. . . But such cities as New York still cry for help. Nearly a century ago Ellen White said that "it is right and proper that means be sent to China. . . But while plans are being carried out to warn the inhabitants of various nations in distant lands, what is being done on behalf of foreigners who have come to the shores of our own land?"

Whereas Ellen White asked the church to reach the foreigners in American cities, if she were alive today she would know that Adventism's large city churches are preponderantly made up of people not native to the United States. While much remains to be done in their ranks, the far greater challenge in

2001 is to reach native-born Americans in the large
cities.[13]

North American Division's World Influence
A Solemn Responsibility

For more than a century the church in North
America viewed seriously the fact that *"God has ordained
the canvassing work"*[14] and thus became a pace-setter in
literature evangelism, a plan which has spread around the
world. Change of traditional economic subsidy support for
qualifying literature evangelists, has resulted in negative
indigenous church growth in western (hard currency) nations.
The church's mission fields today, according to a retired
General Conference officer, are North America, Western
Europe, and Australia.

Even with the strongest of radio and TV electronic
signals, the indigenous western populations are not
responding as desired. "Media will only go so far."[15] "It is
ironic but true that in this age of electronic communications,
personal interaction is becoming more important than ever."[16]
As impressive and dramatic as some evangelistic methods
may be the church must review the counsel of its messenger,
for there is no easy way to win souls.

> *In order to reach all classes, we must meet
> them where they are. They seldom seek us of their
> own accord. Not alone from the pulpit are the hearts
> of men touched by divine truth. There is another field
> of labor, humbler, it may be, but fully as promising. It
> is found in the home of the lowly, and in the mansion
> of the great.*[17] People will be saved one by one.

---

[13] Adventist Review, December 2001, p. 29.
[14] Testimonies, Vol. 6, p. 313, C.M. p. 7.
[15] Adventist Frontiers, January 2003, p. 15.
[16] Regis McKenna
[17] The Desire of Ages, p. 152 (1898), C.M., p. 28.

Lewis Blumenberg, of the New Jersey Conference, stands at the right of a group of his converts at Franklin, New Jersey, church. In the past five years he has delivered more than $100,000.00 worth of literature and has 100 converts. (Photo 1976)

Divine Ratio – 1 to 100

The ministry of such literature evangelists as Lewis E. Blumenberg is an example of God's blessing upon labor for the indigenous. The New Jersey Conference, the Columbia Union Conference, the North American Division, and the world church have each been benefited.

Annual Economic Harvests

For eight years the writer was privileged to serve as publishing department director of the Columbia Union eight-conference territory, he witnessed rich annual harvests of souls from persons of non-Adventist backgrounds.

According to Columbia Union Conference records, in 1975 there were more than 400 converts in that territory from the ministry of full and part-time literature evangelists. In the North American Division 2,368 persons were baptized in 1984 as the result of the ministry of literature evangelists. Such harvests of souls has a positive effect on church finance and may correctly be termed "heavenly economics."

Three Hundred Attend Publishing Convention
Washington, D. C., January 22, 1959

Above are approximately 300 literature evangelists and leaders of the
Columbia Union Conference at the annual convention at Takoma Park, MD.
Convention leaders and principal speakers are shown seated on the front row.
It was a privilege to serve as publishing director of the Columbia Union
Conference for eight years. Columbia Union Literature Evangelists annually
set goals for souls in the hundreds.

Chapter 2 - Begin to Print

Spirit of Prophecy Influence in SDA Publishing

In turning the pages of Seventh-day Adventist denominational history to 1848, we learn of a vision and a Divine Voice speaking to Ellen White. She turned to her husband and said, *"James, I have a message for you. You must <u>begin to print</u> a little paper and send it out to the people. Let it be small at first. . . From this small beginning it was shown to me to be like streams of light that went clear around the world."*[18]

Though limited with funds, they possessed implicit faith. With undaunted courage they began to print the message of the three angels of Revelation 14, before there was a church or conference organization, the total number of adherents to the Advent message numbering only about 100 persons. James White launched a publishing enterprise that was to play an important part in establishing the members of the new movement in the fundamentals of the developing Seventh-day Adventist faith and in welding these adherents into a strong world church.[19]

James White, founder of the Seventh-day Adventist Church. (SDA Encyclopedia, p. 1598)

Divine Guidance

In no way does the church consider the writings of Ellen G. White superior or contrary to the Scriptures; rather, they acknowledge that her counsels relating to organization, temperance, Christian conduct, establishment of a worldwide network of publishing, educational and medical institutions carry great importance.

[18] Life Sketches, p. 125.
[19] Seventh-day Adventist Encyclopedia, pp. 1167,1168.

Next to the Bible, the Spirit of Prophecy is the cohesive element that binds together the Seventh-day Adventist world church in its evangelistic endeavors. In forty years of personal church service the author has observed the influence of the Spirit of Prophecy counsel regarding using the printed page as a principle means of communicating the gospel.

> *Today multiplied thousands of people in many lands sing their Redeemer's praise because in the pages of our books and magazines they first saw the light of present truth, and are now firm and joyful believers in the Advent message.*[20]

"I Have Forgotten His Name"

C. H. Watson, twelfth president of the General Conference, speaks: "The man who sold me a book years ago knows nothing about the effect of that sale. . . I have forgotten his name, but I expect to be in the kingdom because of the sale of that book."[21]

Greatest Wealth of Truth

> *The greatest wealth of truth ever entrusted to mortals, the most solemn and fearful warnings ever sent by God to man, have been committed to them to be given to the world; and in the accomplishment of this work our publishing houses are among the most effective agencies.*[22] *In a large degree through our publishing houses is to be accomplished the work of that other angel who comes down from heaven with great power and who lightens the earth with his glory.*[23]

[20] J. D. Snider.
[21] E. R. Palmer, The Printing Press and the Gospel, p. 145.
[22] Testimonies, Vol. 7, p. 138.
[23] Ibid., p. 140.

Preparing for Reapers

When an evangelist sets up a tent, rents a public hall, is heard on Radio or viewed on TV, and announces that the prophecies of Daniel 2 and Daniel 7 or Revelation 13 will be discussed, strangers whose attention to those topics was first aroused by the visit of a literature evangelist are influenced to respond. Whether or not literature was actually purchased at the time of the visit, gospel seeds were planted. The combined ministries of literature evangelist and pastor compliment each other. "One soweth, another reapeth."

The Backwoods of Wisconsin
"Don't Come on Saturday"

When Tim was a young man, he went into the backwoods of Wisconsin to visit a trapper friend. During the visit the old trapper fell asleep, so Tim looked around the cabin for something to read. He found a book that had pictures of falling stars and some other things that he didn't understand.

A few years later Tim, married and with a family, was invited by a friend to visit his church. In their conversation the friend mentioned the falling of the stars. Tim immediately thought of the old trapper and the book. Again he went into the backwoods to see his trapper friend and found he still had the book, which he didn't want. Tim paid his friend $1.00 for the book, *Bible Readings for the Home Circle*.

When Tim arrived home, he immediately started reading. Before long he was convinced he should become a Seventh-day Adventist. He was baptized and soon family members were also baptized. Tim had twelve children. One son gave Bible studies resulting in the baptism of about thirty people. Another son owned a dairy farm. After he was baptized, he said to the man who came to pick up the milk, "Don't come on Saturday." A friendship was started, and this man and his family were also baptized.

Altogether at least sixty souls were baptized as a result of one young man's reading the book, *Bible Readings*, sold to an old trapper by a literature evangelist.

Most Were Donna's Interests

John Fowler, church administrator, conducted evangelistic meetings in Wyoming with one hundred persons in attendance the first night. Forty of the seventy non-members present had been invited by literature evangelist, Donna Huyck. "Most of the twenty-four people baptized in that meeting were interests of Donna Huyck".[24]

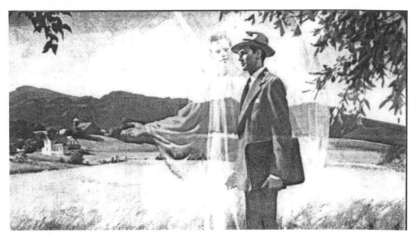

The faithful evangelist who travels from home to home with the pages
of truth can be certain that the angels of God will be round about him,
giving him words to speak; and, in many instances, they go before to
prepare the way and impress the hearts of those who are longing for guidance.

[24] "Literature Evangelist", Nov.-Dec. 1989, p. 4.

The Magic of Communication!

In this hour of electronic surveillance and mass communication advancing at the speed of light, books are being produced, advertised and circulated as never before in human history. Books never die.

> *Books are so old and so familiar as a medium of communication . . . that they are often taken for granted . . . The old magic of communication in books is still without equal . . . Religious books have changed the course of nations, influenced the history of the whole world, and caused millions to turn their allegiance to the God of heaven.*[25]

---

[25] J. D. Snider, I Love Books.

Chapter 3 -
World View of Ellen White

"Get to Know Her."

September 25, 1997 on a coast-to-coast broadcast, Paul Harvey, one of America's most listened-to broadcasters, said:

> I can name an American woman author whose writings have been translated into 148 languages; more than Marx or Tolstoy, more than Agatha Christie, more than William Shakespeare. Only now is the world coming to appreciate her recommended prescription for optimum spiritual and physical health. Ellen White. You don't know her? Get to know her![26]

Kellogg's Cereal City
James and Ellen White

Kellogg's Cereal City in Battle Creek, Michigan, boldly presents the evidence of Ellen White's influence in the history of one of the world's giant breakfast food industries and in the publishing ministry of the Seventh-day Adventist Church. A visit to what may be termed a miniature IMAX at Cereal City is impressive. On a large screen the earth appears as a vast cornfield. Suddenly from the left, two brothers, John Harvey and Will (W. K.) Kellogg, walk into the cornfield scene, bigger than life. From the opposite side Ellen White enters, also appearing bigger than life, and begins conversing with the Kellogg brothers.

Ellen G. White

---

[26] Paul Harvey, on a coast-to-coast broadcast, September 25, 1997.

On the second floor of Cereal City is an ongoing
video that shows James and Ellen White with original copies
of *The Great Controversy* and *Steps to Christ*. In the hall
is a large picture of Ellen White near a picture of W. K.
Kellogg. Significantly, within walking distance of Cereal
City is the house where Ellen White at age thirty-one wrote
The Great Controversy..

How can this be? The world's great cereal king
featuring James and Ellen White! Thousands of visitors who
view these exhibits see Ellen White and her writings featured
along with Dr. John Harvey Kellogg's Battle Creek treatment
equipment. This is of special interest and reassurance to
Seventh-day Adventists regarding the important role of the
church's messenger. It also indicates recognition of the
power and influence of the press.

The Whites and W. K. Kellogg

Biographer Horace B. Powell speaks of James and
Ellen White in the book, *The Original has this Signature, W.
K. Kellogg*, printed in 1956 by Prentice Hall. His preface
states,
> . . . so – this is the story of the Seventh-day
> Adventists whose ideas on health reform made Battle
> Creek the cereal food capitol of the world.

The food industry grew up in Battle Creek
because the Sanitarium was there. The Sanitarium
was there because Elder and Sister White and the
Adventists established it there. The history of W. K.
Kellogg and the corn flakes business is rooted in the
history of the Seventh-day Adventist denomination.
. . Rooted in the influence of this (SDA) movement.
. . he always spoke of them as "our people" and
the injunctions of the church during his formative,

impressionable years made indelible marks upon
him.[27]

The Book *The Great Controversy*

Above Silver or Gold – *The Great Controversy
should be widely circulated. It contains the story
of the past, the present and the future. In its outline
of the closing scenes of this earth's history, it bears
a powerful testimony in behalf of the truth. I am
more anxious to see a wide circulation for this book
than for any other I have written; for in The Great
Controversy, the last message of warning is given
more distinctly than in any other of my books.*[28]

Some years ago at a conference in London, England,
Evangelist F. A. Spearing told of a conversation he had with
a gentleman who was a "reader" for a prestigious publishing
house in London. An expert on manuscripts and books, the
gentleman, Mr. A., had read *The Great Controversy* lent him
by his landlady. He asked Mr. Spearing, "Did Mrs. White
really write this book?"

Spearing replied, "She certainly did."

"Was she an educated woman?" Mr. A. questioned.

"No," Spearing answered, "Not as the term is
commonly understood."

"Well," Mr. A. said, "it is a wonderful book. It is
almost perfect in composition. I have read thousands of
manuscripts, but none more beautiful than this book."[29]

W. A. Spicer, president of the General Conference of
Seventh-day Adventists from 1922 to 1930, said, "Well do I

[27] Horace B. Powell, The Original Has This Signature, p. 18.
[28] Ellen G. White letter 281, 1905, C.M., p. 127.
[29] W. A. Spicer, Pioneer Days of the Advent Message, p. 193.

remember how this book [*The Great Controversy*] thrilled and convicted my youthful heart as I sat up nearly all one night to read it when the first edition came from the press in the early eighties."[30]

It was a copy of *The Great Controversy* that led the author's mother, a Methodist, to join the Seventh-day Adventist Church.

Just What I've Been Looking For

A young man took his family on a vacation and rented a timeshare for a week. In the timeshare there were some books. One particular book caught the young man's eye. It was *The Great Controversy* bought from an unknown literature evangelist, and left in the timeshare by the owner. As he read this book the young man said to his wife, "This is just what I have been looking for. It gives the answers to all my questions about what is going on and what will happen." The family of four was brought into the Seventh-day Adventist church by that one book. The two children are now attending church school. How many will be in heaven due to one literature evangelist and one book? No one really knows.[31]

Answering Questions People Are Asking

Dr. R. W. Browning is now a faithful member of the Greenwood, Mississippi, Seventh-day Adventist church. How did this happen? He never knowingly met a Seventh-day Adventist until he wrote requesting to become a member. He did this after he was given a used copy of *The Great Controversy*, sold decades before by a literature evangelist.[32]

[30] Ibid, p. 193.
[31] E-mail from Willard Hackett, 22 April 2003.
[32] Southern Tidings, December, 1999.

Some who buy the books will lay them on the shelf or place them on the parlor table and seldom look at them. Still, God has a care for His truth, and the time will come when these books will be sought for and read.[33]

The Great Controversy is **still relevant** for today, answering questions people are asking.

"That's It, I've Got to Have That Book!"

Yahilia Gomez, a student at Greater Miami Adventist Academy worked with the MagaBook program during the summer. She will never forget a man who answered the door and told her if she was selling Christian literature he was not interested, and slammed the door. In a few minutes the same man came running down the street asking her to come back to his house. With some apprehension she did. He said, "Show me all the books you have. After you left a voice spoke to me and said I need a book you have, and I was shown a vision of it." As she pulled the books from her bag, he looked at each one intently. When she showed him *The Great Controversy*, he said, "That is it! I've got to have that book!"[34]

Destruction in New York City

Men and nations have become angry. Much of society is out of control. On September 11, 2001, when the experiences in this book were first being compiled, angry men from Middle East countries with specially crafted knives hijacked U. S. aircraft and brought down two of the world's tallest structures, the twin towers of the World Trade Center in New York City. Almost three thousand lives were lost.

[33]Testimonies, Vol. 6, pp. 313,314. (1900), C.M., p. 150.
[34] Southern Tidings, December, 1999.

Middle East Hospitality

Yet, in 1954 the writer traveled overland through
Moslem lands of Pakistan, Iran, Iraq, Lebanon and Syria,
where he was treated with royal kindness, reminiscent of
Abraham's treatment of strangers. At Zihedan, Iran a Persian
Major, in charge of military affairs for much of Iran, invited
our family to spend the night at his comfortable home located
on military grounds. Before we rolled out our bedrolls to
retire in a room carpeted wall to wall with Persian rugs, he
and his lovely wife served us fruit, nuts and refreshing drink
in another room where they enjoyed leisure moments. The
following morning as we left on the bus the Major embraced
me, kissing both cheeks in traditional style, then through a
translator said it was like telling a brother goodbye.

Stories of hospitality and friendliness extended to the
family as they traveled without reservations through Bible
lands on a ten thousand-mile, 90-day journey are recorded in
the author's book entitled *Bold Journey*.

New York City's Helpless Firemen

In 1904 Ellen White envisioned dangers with the
construction of New York City's tall buildings. She said,
*"When I was last in New York, I was in the night season
called upon to behold buildings rising story after story
toward heaven. These buildings were warranted to be
fireproof. . . .*

*"The scene that next passed before me was an
alarm of fire. . . The fire engines could do nothing to stay
the destruction. The firemen were unable to operate the
engines. "*[35] Does this sound familiar?

---

[35] Life Sketches, p. 413

Eighty years ago Arthur S. Maxwell, well-known Adventist author, wrote regarding the vulnerability of New York City's tall buildings. In his book is a picture of New York City skyscrapers, with a seaplane flying above the city, inscribed as follows: "Seaplane flying over New York, illustrating the awful possibilities of destruction by bombing aircraft."[36]

[36] Arthur S. Maxwell, This Mighty Hour, Stanborough Press Ltd., 1933, p. 92.

Chapter 4 -
A Century and a Half of Seed Sowing

We rejoice in reports of large soul-winning harvests. Presently the most glowing reports are of mega-evangelist campaigns conducted by evangelists from western nations, working in developing nations where for nearly a century literature evangelists have worked preparing for today's harvests.

According to the "law of the harvest," there must first be seed-sowing, then the harvest. For many decades the church has been publishing and literature evangelists have been circulating the message of the three angels, "like the leaves of autumn." *"Our publications are now sowing the gospel seed, and are instrumental in bringing as many souls to Christ as the preached word."*[37]

"Both Workers Have Light" "The ministerial evangelist who engages in the canvassing work is performing a service fully as important as that of preaching the gospel before a congregation Sabbath after Sabbath." *Letter 186, 1903. Colporteur Ministry, p. 45* Illustration by Vernon Herod

"More than a thousand will be converted in a day, most of whom will trace their first conviction to the reading of our publications."[38]

Heaven places a high regard on the canvassing ministry. *"God has ordained the canvassing work. . . All who consecrate themselves to God to work as canvassers are assisting to give the last message of warning to the world."* [39]

With divine assurance, laymen, convicted of the need to spread the gospel, separate

---

[37] Review and Herald, June 10, 1880, C.M. p. 150.
[38] Review and Herald, Nov. 10, 1885, C.M. p. 151
[39] Test. Vol. 6, p. 313. (1900) C.M. pp. 6, 7.

themselves from secular employment to become literature evangelists, certain that ". . . *God looks upon the faithful evangelistic canvasser with as much approval as He looks upon any faithful minister. Both workers have light, and both are to shine in their respective spheres of influence.*"[40] Both are guided by Scripture and Spirit of Prophecy. Evidence of divine direction of the Lord's Messenger in the publishing ministry of the Seventh-day Adventist church is unmistakable.

Denominational Recognition

Literature Evangelist — A *Seventh-day Adventist who regularly sells from house-to-house denominational books and magazines to the public. He is considered a gospel worker whose efforts are coordinated with those of the other evangelistic workers of the church. His work is a sacred one, and partakes of that of a minister, a teacher, and a salesman.*[41]

"*The efficient colporteur [literature evangelist] as well as the minister should have a sufficient remuneration for his/her services if his/her work is faithfully done.*"[42]

"*The literature evangelist receives a commission on his sales and also certain financial benefits if he meets stipulated requirements set forth in denominational policies.*"[43]

"**As Important as Preaching**. The ministerial evangelist who engages in the canvassing work is performing a service fully as important as that of preaching the gospel before a congregation Sabbath after Sabbath."[44]

[40] Ellen G. White letter 186, 1903, C.M., p. 45.
[41] Seventh-day Adventist Encyclopedia, p. 791.
[42] Testimonies, Vol. 4, pp. 389, 390 (1880), C.M., p. 28.
[43] Seventh-day Adventist Encyclopedia, p. 792.
[44] Ellen G. White letter 186, 1903.

For a layman to respond to the call of the Lord and the call of His church to become a literature evangelist, requires faith, undaunted courage and commitment.

Why Be a Literature Evangelist?

Literature evangelists like the children of Issachar *"have understanding of the times to know what Israel ought to do."*[45] The church provides each literature evangelist with a license or credential identifying him/her as representing a special ministry of the Seventh-day Adventist church. Though literature evangelism is not an easy work, it is highly rewarding in soul winning, and indeed economically, to the church.

Bravely They Go – Anywhere, Anytime

For years Catholics and Protestants have been locked in unholy political and religious turmoil in Ireland. While the author was conducting a literature evangelist institute in Ireland it was not unusual to hear exploding bombs.

Literature evangelist Tony Brownlow, fearless for his Master, worked in areas both Protestant and Catholic where during years of political unrest, hundreds of persons had been murdered or killed by bombings. Officers of opposing factions respected Tony Brownlow's ministry. He was allowed passage to cither area. Listen as this brave man tells of his work.

God Blesses Even in Political Turmoil

"The Lord has blessed me beyond measure, and in strange times. Even tonight (Saturday) in a home on the

[45] I Chronicles 12:32

Catholic Creggan Estate, bullets barely missed a lady by half
an inch as she nursed her baby. This happened just minutes
before I called on her. My next call was in Bogside, where
the lady of the house said that her husband was in Long Kesh
Prison. Nearly all my Christmas deliveries were in Catholic
areas that were participating in the Rent strike, and yet 98%
of my books delivered."

In writing to Pastor John Arthur, now Publishing
Director of the Trans European Division, Brother Brownlow
said: "A young soldier was killed today. Just a few days ago
he was sitting in an easy chair in our living room. The house
where we lived in Londonderry had the glass shattered by a
bomb in our back bedroom."

Count the Dots

The accompanying map is an example of world
coverage by literature evangelism. Each dot represents

contact by
student literature
evangelists in just
one county in one
summer in the
Southern Union,
North American
Division. Sixty-
seven years ago six
students engaged
1,167 persons in
personal spiritual
exchange, leaving
in their trail copies
of *Our Day in the
Light of Prophecy*

January 16, 1936-- "What would happen if?"   and *Bible Readings for the Home Circle.*[46]

The work of these six students provides insight into the careful, thorough ministry of literature evangelists. These six students, working in just one county in Carolina, brought gospel light to 1,167 homes. Without question some of these persons who bought books and/or were enrolled in Bible Studies were moved by the Holy Spirit to accept the Three Angels' Messages and for long years have strengthened the church with sons and daughters, tithes and offerings. God's promises are absolute. Sow the seed. There will be a harvest!

During the past sixty-seven years as one generation passes away and another generation enters the scene, students, full-time and part-time literature evangelists continue to criss-cross this same area selling more and more books to more and more people. No generation or area of earth is knowingly left untouched by literature evangelists.

Ultimate Commitment

It is easy to say, "Lord, hasten Your coming." To say, "Here am I, Lord send me," is another thing.

Some years ago Walla Walla College Press Manager, John Wohlers told me about his literature evangelist father, William Herman (W. H. or Will) Wohlers and his deep commitment to his divine calling made evident by his final request. "On a table next to my casket," he said, "place a display of the books I have been selling. They bear the Three Angels' Messages for the world." His last sales demonstration reflected his commitment to his Maker. *"Seest thou a man diligent in his business? he shall stand before kings; he shall not stand before mean men."* [47]

During approximately forty years which the author

[46] General Church Paper of the Seventh-day Adventists, Takoma Park, Wash. DC, Jan. 16, 1936
[47] Proverbs 22:29.

was privileged to spend in the publishing ministry of the church he has been impressed with children who grow up in homes of faithful, dedicated and disciplined literature evangelist families. Such families provide stability important to the church. The influence of committed parents builds strength of character into the lives of succeeding generations. Stories of literature evangelist families reveal that a large percentage of their sons and daughters become involved in life-long major ministries of the church, many in the field of education, holding loyally to church beliefs.

Bible Readings for the Home Circle

The book *Bible Readings* originally had as part of its title *for the Home Circle*. Contributed by a large number of Bible scholars, it contains 200 sermons written in question and answer form. Sold first in 1884, copyrighted in 1915, it has been circulated by literature evangelists across America and around the world. The spiritual influence of this evangelistic masterpiece is phenomenal. Conversion stories are legion.

Charles D. Brooks,
General Conference World
Evangelist.

Peggy Tompkins, wife of retired church administrator Elder Joel Tompkins, tells that a copy of *Bible Readings* purchased many years ago from a literature evangelist in England, brought the Three Angels' Messages to her family.

The boyhood home of Pastor Charles D. Brooks, retired General Conference evangelist, was in North Carolina. He tells the following story of how the Seventh-day Adventist message was brought to his family:

When I was an infant Mother was impressed to keep the seventh-day Sabbath. For several years we did not know anyone else who was keeping the Sabbath.

One day my eldest sister heard a knock at the door. There stood literature evangelist Willie White. He began describing the book he was selling, entitled *Bible Readings*. After listening for a short time she said that she was not interested in religious discussions because the truth was not taught or practiced in churches today.

Willie White asked what she meant. My sister replied, "Ministers and churches do not teach obedience to God's Ten Commandments. We are not worshipping God on the true Sabbath. The Bible says the seventh day is the Sabbath, and that day is not Sunday."

Willie White smiled and asked, "Would you like to attend a church where everybody believes like you do?" The next day the pastor of the Seventh-day Adventist church visited our home, and on Saturday, seven members of our family went to that church. I was a small boy, but I shall never forget my conviction that we had found the Truth. A few weeks later we were baptized.

Because literature evangelist Willie White contacted us, today many of my relatives are members of the Seventh-day Adventist Church. They are Bible workers, nurses, schoolteachers, church elders and officers.

In my ministry it has been my privilege to

baptize more than 12,500 persons into the Seventh-day Adventist church. All this began when literature evangelist Willie White knocked at the door of my sister's home. [48]

In heaven where redeemed souls are counted instead of dollars Willie White will be considered a star literature evangelist.

Seventy Years Ago in Saskatchewan

The Lake Union Conference is thankful for the soul-winning ministry of a mother and daughter whose combined years of canvassing totaled sixty-two, with hundreds enrolled in Bible studies. The story began seventy years ago in Tinsdale, Saskatchewan, Canada when a literature evangelist sold a copy of *Bible Readings for the Home Circle* to the grandparents of Burniece Goetz Walters. When Burniece was about three years old, her father took the family to Saskatchewan to meet his parents. It was wintertime. During their stay temperatures dipped to 40 degrees below zero. On days like that the family stayed inside and entertained themselves as best they could.

One day as Burniece's mother, Florence, wandered through the house, she discovered the *Bible Readings* book in the bookcase. Florence had not been raised a Christian but on occasion had visited an aunt who was a Seventh-day Adventist. She had not given much thought to religion. However, on this cold day she spent hours devouring the message in the book, carefully comparing it with the Bible. After reading and studying she gave her heart to the Lord.

When the family returned to Michigan, Florence joined the Seventh-day Adventist Church. Soon her mother, her brother, and the brother's family became interested in the

[48]Story received from C. D. Brooks, January 7, 2002.

message and joined the church. Florence raised ten children
as Seventh-day Adventists, gave Bible studies to neighbors
and shared tracts with people she contacted.

After her last child entered school, Florence began a
career in literature evangelism which continued for twenty
years. Most of her 130 descendants are members of the
Seventh-day Adventist Church.

In Mother's Footsteps

Florence's daughter, Burniece, also chose literature
evangelism as her life work. Burniece knows of at least 120
people who have joined the Adventist Church through her
literature evangelism contacts. During her last year of work
she enrolled 140 persons in Bible courses.

Burniece looked after family members. For many
years she and her husband transported her sister's eight
children nearly one hundred miles round trip to attend
Sabbath School each week. The children had no other way.
The Goetz family themselves lived within walking distance
of their church. "It's the best missionary work we ever did,"
Burniece said. "All but one of the children are in the church
today."[49]

Imagine the joy awaiting the Canadian church
member who left secular employment to become a literature
evangelist, when he learns the results of the sale of just one
copy of *Bible Readings*.

From Homeless Lad to Publishing Director

In the city of Bogotá, Colombia, many homeless
children live on the streets. They forage for their food. On

[49] Lake Union Herald, July 1989, p. 3.

cold nights some sleep over warm exhaust vents of large stores. A concerned Seventh-day Adventist lady found one such lad, took him to her home, fed and clothed him, and gave him a loving home and a good education. In reporting the story the late Pastor Joe Hunt said, "A few weeks ago I met the boy, now a young man. He is a publishing leader in Colombia with ten assistant leaders under his care. He is a vibrant, enthusiastic giant for God."

Like the Sands of the Sahara

The author and his wife lived in England for six years. In preparing to leave for his office one morning, he noticed the car was covered with a fine dust. He went back into the house and said, "Our car is covered with Sahara Desert dust!" The morning newspaper verified that as a fact. Tons of Sahara Desert sand, borne on the wings of the wind had traveled thousands of miles, dusting villages, cities, the countryside and ships at sea.

Similarly since the days of George King, "apostle of the canvassing work"[50] literature evangelists have, like the floating sands of the Sahara, fanned out across the face of the earth, knocking on doors, calling from gates, doing a work unparalleled in Seventh-day Adventist door-to-door ministry. Literature evangelists are like John the Baptist, forerunner of the Saviour. *"With vision illuminated by the Divine Spirit, he studied the characters of men, that he might understand how to reach their hearts with the message of heaven."*[51] Wherever the feet of bookmen tread there is light – "streams of light that will encircle the earth."[52]

[50] W. A. Spicer, Story of the Advent Message, (1881), p. 89.
[51] Test. Vol. 8, p. 222.
[52] Life Sketches, p. 125, C.M., p. 1.

Union of Human and Divine

If ever one among us suggests that because of world conditions "you can't knock on strangers' doors," these are not words of the brave. It must be understood that there is no limit to the power of the Holy Spirit. Throughout denominational publishing history methods of approach have been tailored to adapt to different personalities, to changing times, and to varying circumstances. While people struggle spiritually and intellectually for answers, the Seventh-day Adventist Church dares not become complacent or too comfortable.

It Happened in Singapore

One day in Singapore in 1949 a young father was riding in a bicycle taxi with a small casket at his feet and a shovel at his side. He was traveling toward the low ridges overlooking the weapon-cluttered beach. There he would bury the child of his fond affection. The author saw this young father and tried to imagine his questions about life: Why war? Why death? Is there something better in the future?

Somehow I knew that one of the literature evangelists of Singapore would one day knock on this man's door with answers to his questions.

Chapter 5 -
Divine Economics -- An Untold Story

A careful examination of church world growth indicates that a large percentage of souls won can be attributed to the literature ministry.

British Literature Evangelist Arthur Morgan, illustrates the use of a sales aid.

Church records contain the names of thousands of converts from the direct and indirect ministry of literature evangelists resulting in families and their descendants who today are supporting and guiding the church throughout the world.

Joseph Bates, a Colporteur

Joseph Bates, a colporteur.

"It was in 1839 that Adventist pioneer, Joseph Bates, heard the first lectures on the coming of the Lord. He had retired from the sea, and the former captain was owner of a little farm two and a half miles from New Bedford, Massachusetts.

"In the earliest testimony from any of our brethren, we see Joseph Bates as a colporteur. He was a literature worker all his life."[53]

Blacksmith H. S. Gurney said, "In 1840 Elder Joseph Bates

[53]W. A. Spicer, Pioneer Days of the Advent Movement, pp. 130, 131.

came into my shop with the first number of the *Advent
Herald*, published in Boston, Massachusetts by Elder J. V.
Himes. He was getting subscribers for the paper. It was just
what I wanted."[54]

Finland's Laymen – Aflame for God

Secular history records great bravery by four million
Finnish people in defending their nation against 180 million
Russians in 1939.[55] Today that same courage is equally
effective in proclaiming the gospel of love.

In 1966 when the writer visited beautiful Sumi
Finland to conduct literature evangelist institutes he
experienced some of the coldest weather he had ever known.
Upon arrival he was told to either purchase a seal skin hat or
freeze. That seal skin hat proved to be the most expensive
and warmest hat I ever owned!

Eighty-six members of Finland's publishing family, 1971 — Literature
Evangelists, publishing house workers and publishing leaders.
(Anna Lisa Helevaara, first row, second from right, wearing glasses.)

The writer found literature evangelists of Finland

[54] Ibid., p. 130.
[55] Condon, Richard W., The Winter War, p. 7.

among some of earth's most dedicated and energetic workers. They have placed tens of thousand of books and journals in the homes of this geographically small country. Over 140,000 sets of Uncle Arthur's *The Bible Story* have been sold in Finland. **Ten thousand** sets of *The Bible Story* have been placed in the city of Tampere alone. Imagine! There are more sets of Bible Stories in Finland than there are Sauna baths!

A sense of urgency led Anna-Lisa Helevaara, a former Communist, to contact people of all classes. She declares, "We have a message and the world must hear it quickly." The author was told that during one year she placed more than 850 complete ten-volume sets of Uncle Arthur's *The Bible Story* in full color with families in her assigned territory.

Erkki Mottus

Another of Finland's highly successful literature evangelists, Erkki Mottus, delivered 830 copies of *The Great Controversy* during the year 1969.[56]

The writer's memory of the publishing program in Finland is of a well-equipped and well-managed publishing house directed by young people, with an impressive program of field promotion and distribution of gospel literature. Sales promotion is the lifeblood of the church's prophetic publishing ministry, ensuring stability for its publishing houses. One publishing house manager stated, 'You can't cook a meal if you let the fire go out."

---

[56] Illustrated Statistical Report Finland Publishing House, Kirjatoimi, 1897-1972

From Student Literature Evangelist to Preacher

This story tells of a never-ending river of soul-winning and economic strength which began seventy-four years ago in South Dakota with J. A. Estey. Once a rough character, he met his Lord and surrendered his life for service. He had an eighth-grade education. He wanted to train for the ministry, so must go to school. To earn his way to attend academy, he canvassed during summer months.

When Estey finished the academy, he felt the burden to preach. His conference told him they had no preaching position open. They suggested that he become a literature evangelist. He worked long hours successfully canvassing that summer.

General Conference, union and local conference publishing department directors of the North American Division in 1964, pictured with officers of the General Conference, union and local conferences.

During his student canvassing experience, Estey learned how to convincingly present the gospel and persuade human minds. As fall came, he launched out on his own to hold two series of evangelistic meetings near Bison, South Dakota.

The area around Bison was sparsely settled except for a few buffalo, coyotes and oversized jack rabbits. Out on the prairie, a number of miles from town lived Wallace Claridge with his wife and six children. Wallace and his family attended Estey's evangelistic meetings. They accepted the Adventist message and were baptized, as was another family who owned a large neighboring farm. A church group was soon organized, and J. A. Estey built a church building.

Christian education becomes important with the message of Adventism. Consequently the children of Wallace Claridge and his wife were educated in Adventist schools. They grew up, married and established families of their own far away from the prairies of South Dakota. The oldest son, John, and his wife owned a nursing home in Washington State. After retirement they participated in thirty-seven Maranatha projects. They still volunteer. The second son, Wallace, owned a printing business in Colorado. Charles became a dentist, David a teacher, and Lawrence a teacher and builder. Daughter, Betty, taught in Seventh-day Adventist schools. The six children have remained committed Adventists, giving their tithes, offerings, their families and their lives to fulfill the gospel commission.

The second generation children, twenty-one in number, have become teachers, nurses, doctors, printers, medical workers, and businessmen and women who remain loyal and supportive of the church. This loyalty is now being passed on to the succeeding generation.

Speaking of the economic returns from the work of one literature evangelist turned preacher, one of the Claridge brothers said, "Our family has put **millions** into the church." [57]

Gospel to the World

Our church history is replete with gospel adventures of often lone literature evangelists who opened doors to the gospel both at home and in distant lands. When one searches the Seventh-day Adventist Encyclopedia country by country,

[57]This story told to the author by the oldest Claridge brother, John, in May 2001.

he will discover that, with rare exception, the pathway for the Seventh-day Adventist Church and its world missions was pioneered by literature evangelists preparing the way for the preacher.

Literature evangelists took the message of the Three Angels to South America and to the Orient, the Philippines, China, and Indonesia. For nearly a century literature evangelists have accomplished much in Africa and India.

Publishing House for Indonesia

In 1948 when the writer arrived in the beautiful Dutch East Indies, now Indonesia, commercial printers were printing Seventh-day Adventist subscription literature. Their production schedules were unreliable for a fast-growing army of literature evangelists whose livelihood depended on an uninterrupted flow of literature. When Seventh-day Adventist world church treasurer, C. L. Torrey, visited the Dutch East Indies, I explained our production problem. The result was a Thirteenth Sabbath Overflow Offering assigned to build the Indonesian Publishing House.

"Bekin Buka Pinto Ke Sorga" – Make Open the Door to Heaven - The Cry of Humanity

It happened in Java, Indonesia in 1948 at the time when 400 years of Dutch colonialism was harshly brought to an end. In an hour of political turmoil when the Dutch were losing a beautiful island empire and the Indonesians regaining their sovereignty, an evangelistic meeting conducted by Ralph Watts, Sr. was held in the large, beautiful Concordia Hall in the heart of Bandung, known as the City of Flowers.

The audience was made up of both Dutch and Indonesians each anxious for an understanding of a perplexing hour of history. Seats in the hall were filled and overflowing. People were sitting in the wide windowsills. Firemen closed the massive two-leaf doors against the pressing crowd trying to gain entrance.

People outside began pounding on the great doors calling loudly, "**Bekin Buka Pinto Ke Sorga!**" "**Make Open the Door to Heaven!**"   I heard their cry. It is the cry of the world. It is the cry that impresses laymen to leave their "nets" and lay up treasure in heaven.

Adventist Beginnings in India

Today's impressive soul winning harvests in India may be traced to the planting of gospel seed in the form of the printed page by literature evangelists in the 1890s. In 1893 Willard Lenker and A. T. Stroup, two colporteurs from America, began selling Seventh-day Adventist subscription books among the English-speaking inhabitants of the major cities. In 1894 workers from Australia joined the colporteurs from America, and work was continued in the cities of Madras, Mysore, Hyderabad and Calcutta. During this time people were asking that books be translated into the local languages. This was done as early as 1894. It is interesting to note that a pamphlet prepared by S. N. Haskell on the life of Christ, was translated and published by an independent Protestant mission in Poona, India in 1894.[58]

Three Angels Message to China

It was wintertime in Northern California, and retired seaman, Abram LaRue, was standing behind a large heating stove with his back to the stovepipe that extended up through

---

[58] Seventh-day Adventist Encyclopedia., p. 625.

the ceiling. For the sake of economy, walls in the room had been papered with Adventist missionary literature. As he faced the nearby wall, he read mission appeals of need for the gospel to be taken to China. As his body was being warmed, so was his heart. He would respond to that need. His conscience would not allow him to remain warm and comfortable – not with China waiting for the gospel.

He sent a letter to the General Conference indicating his willingness to go to China. In response the General Conference expressed appreciation and inquired regarding his age. Upon learning of La Rue's advanced age, they carefully worded a letter, thanking him for his desire and willingness to serve as a missionary to China, then kindly informed him that the church did not send missionaries overseas at his age.

LaRue's quick reply was, "Don't worry about my age. My health is above normal." After a continued exchange of letters the answer was still, "No."

In a final letter Abraham LaRue requested permission to go as a missionary to some small island in the Pacific. General Conference leaders, respecting his persistence, relented, thinking he would perhaps choose one of the Hawaiian Islands. As a seaman Abram LaRue had knowledge of oceans, land masses and earth's islands. To the surprise of General Conference leaders, he chose the island of Hong Kong, a ten-minute ferry ride from the mainland of China – his goal realized.

When Abram LaRue went to Hong Kong in 1888 he set up a seamen's mission. For fourteen years he did colporteur work, mainly on the ships in the Hong Kong harbor. During that time he also sailed out of Hong Kong harbor on ships going to Shanghai, Japan, Borneo, Java, Ceylon, Sarawak, Singapore, and once to Palestine and Lebanon, selling books and distributing tracts wherever his ship stopped.[59]

[59] Seventh-day Adventist Encyclopedia, p. 764.

Along with his work in Hong Kong for Europeans, he also circulated tracts in Chinese, translated for him by a Chinese friend.[60] "This humble messenger of the cross was the actual forerunner of the large work that later developed in China."[61] The Shanghai Publishing House was established and scores of colporteurs and evangelists were soon working. "Brother LaRue lived to see the truth take root in this land as he introduced the message through the printed page."[62]

Until his death in Hong Kong Abram LaRue was a man of tireless energy. The writer visited his resting place where he awaits the call of the life-giver.

Literature Ministry to Japan

Japan Union Literature Evangelist Institute—1953

Abraham LaRue went to Yokahoma, Japan in 1889 where he distributed Adventist publications.[63] Although World War II briefly slowed Seventh-day Adventist work in Japan, the various ministries of the church are highly

[60] Ibid., p. 764
[61] Palmer, E. R., The Printing Press and the Gospel, p. 143 (W.H.Branson)
[62] Ibid., p. 143.
[63] Seventh-day Adventist Encyclopedia, p. 700.

evident today. Presently there are more than 200 literature
evangelists in Japan.[64]

Armstrong, Japan

Elder Victor T. Armstrong was president of the Japan
Union Mission of Seventh-day Adventists. One day he
received a letter addressed simply: ARMSTRONG, JAPAN.

The letter was from the son of a sea captain who had
received a book many years earlier when his ship stopped
in Hong Kong. As the captain read the book, he was
convinced that the seventh day is the Sabbath. He shared
his faith with others on his remote island . Many joined
him in worshipping on the Bible Sabbath. The captain was
certain there must be a group of believers somewhere who
worship on the seventh day. As ships visited his island, he
went aboard to inquire if anyone knew of people keeping the
seventh day Sabbath.

After the captain's death his son took up the quest.
One day a ship captain told of a missionary in Japan named
Armstrong. A letter was sent bearing only one name and one
country ! – ARMSTRONG, JAPAN. An alert postal worker
guided by Providence delivered the letter to Elder Victor
Armstrong's office. Soon Elder Armstrong and a Japanese
pastor traveled by ocean freighter to the distant island where
they met with a group of Sabbath-keeping believers.

Only eternity will reveal the far reaching results of
Abram LaRue's placement of message-laden books by land
and sea. Today's Global Mission and Adventist Frontier
Mission workers, serving in the islands and lands afar, follow
the footsteps of Abram LaRue.

[64] Information from General Conference Publishing Department, June 18, 2004.

Don't Send it, I Want to See You

Fukuinsha, the Seventh-day Adventist Publishing

House in Japan, produces an eleven volume Spirit of Prophecy set, including the Conflict of the Ages series, *Christ's Object Lessons*, and other Ellen G. White books.

Literature Evangelists of the Island of Guam—1952

They also produce the Japanese *Signs* magazine, nearly 50,000 copies each month. One reader who continues to subscribe wrote, "Please don't send my magazine by mail. Bring it – I want to see you." Another requested that the magazine be sent to his office, not to his house, because "my little girl cuts the pictures out of it."[65]

Personal Contact

Mrs. Komura Udaka, one of Japan's oldest literature evangelists is eighty-six years old. She has been an active, licensed literature evangelist for over forty years. During 1993 she visited 1,787 homes, selling magazines and books, distributing tracts and giving Bible studies to sixty-nine people. [66]

Community Service to the Rescue

While living in Singapore, it was the author's privilege to meet annually with Japan's literature evangelists. To go from tropical Singapore to Japan in wintertime was

[65 & 66] Information by Russell Thomas, Far Eastern Division Publishing Director in 1994.

an educational experience. A lightweight tropical suit worn
in Singapore was inadequate for Japanese weather. Elder
Marvin Reeder, then publishing director of the Japan Union,
immediately took the author to the Dorcas Center (Adventist
Community Service), where adequate winter clothing was
provided . Especially appreciated was a pair of long winter
underwear. Needless to say, the author has deep respect for
the church's Community Service program.

> *"Sing unto the Lord a new song, and His*
> *praise from the end of the earth, ye that go down*
> *to the sea, and all that is therein; the isles, and the*
> *inhabitants thereof." Isaiah 42:10.*

> *"He shall not fail nor be discouraged, till he*
> *have set judgment in the earth: and the isles shall*
> *wait for his law." Isaiah 42:4.*

The King is Coming

In 1969 while conducting a Literature Evangelist
Institute at our Seventh-day Adventist college in Ethiopia, the
author was privileged to meet the greatly respected Emperor
Haile Selassie when he made a visit to that school.

For three days prior to the Emperor's visit, there was
extensive preparation by faculty and students. Buildings
were cleaned and painted. Schoolroom desks were taken
out of doors, washed, and polished. The boys pressed their
trousers. The girls curled their hair. Students practiced the
Ethiopian National Anthem and a gospel hymn to sing for
their Emperor.

On the day of the royal visit, students and faculty
began watching the entry gate leading from the highway into
the school grounds. Upon arrival the Emperor said to his

armour guard, "Be at ease. It is safe here."

Nationals living nearby were happy to learn of the Emperor's visit. On that day his people lined the highway, anxious to see and wave to the Emperor as he passed by in his Rolls Royce. They wanted to see and hoped to touch him. Often along his travel route he threw gifts to admiring persons. Among those who waited were the blind and crippled, longing for help.

After the Emperor's visit there were still the blind, the crippled, and the maimed.

How different when King Jesus visited villages. *"And Jesus went about all Galilee, teaching in their synagogues, and preaching the gospel of the kingdom, and healing all manner of sickness, and all disease among the people."*[67]

Haile Selassie's housekeeper, Mrs. Hanson, was a Seventh-day Adventist. The emperor subscribed to *Life and Health* magazine. After receiving and reading each issue, he would give a health lecture/synopsis to Mrs. Hanson.

The Emperor was greatly pleased when the ten-volume *The Bible Story* set was printed in his Amharic language.

Ethiopia and Ethiopians are mentioned several times in the Scriptures. In Psalm 68:31 we read that ". . . *Ethiopia shall soon stretch out her hands unto God.*" This they have done.

---

[67] Matthew 4:23.

Chapter 6 - Voice of Prophecy and Literature Evangelists

Elder H. M. S. Richards, Sr.

In 1926 over radio station KNX in Los Angeles, California, Elder H.M.S. Richards, Sr. introduced his marvelous radio ministry. In a few years the Voice of Prophecy radio broadcast became a regular feature. In 1942 Elder Richards introduced the Voice of Prophecy Bible Correspondence School.[68]

Elder H. M. S. Richards, founder of Voice of Prophecy radio evangelism.

Elder Richards was a regular attendee at Literature Evangelist Conventions, giving vigorous support to literature evangelism, knowing that in home visitations interest is awakened in minds of strangers concerning matters eternal. Such persons are excellent prospects for the Voice of Prophecy Bible Course and, ultimately, church fellowship.

As of 1974 total VOP Bible School enrollments numbered 1,577,782.[69] At one time Elder Richards told the writer that 50% of VOP enrollments came from literature evangelists.

The Voice of Prophecy ministry has a compelling sixty-two year soul-winning history. Souls brought into church fellowship from initial literature evangelist Voice of Prophecy Bible Course enrollment contacts may not always be traced or credited to their ministry. However, the record

---

[68] Seventh-day Adventist Encyclopedia, p. 1558.
[69] Ibid., p. 1561.

of Voice of Prophecy soul-winning success recommends encouragement and expansion of the ministry of literature evangelists.

> As the books he [a literature evangelist] is leaving in the homes are read and studied, many are led into fuller understanding, spiritual conviction, and then into church fellowship through the influence of the press. Thousands of people who become interested in the SDA teachings first in this way enroll in Bible correspondence schools or attend evangelistic meetings and become members of the SDA Church.[70]

Bible School Enrollments Aboard Boeing 707

After hearing the Voice of Prophecy Radio program and studying the Bible Correspondence Course, John became a Seventh-day Adventist. In 1972 he visited H. M. S. Richards at the VOP headquarters.

The indomitable John Curnow, author of "Death on Dark Wings" (his WWII experience) and former Publishing Director of the Southern Asia Division, was at one time manager of a vast tea plantation in India with 3,000 employees. One night while listening to his short-wave radio, his attention was attracted to a Voice of Prophecy program. He was impressed to take the Bible Correspondence Course, which led to his baptism and a life in literature evangelism.

It was a privilege for the author to travel with Pastor Curnow through his territory on India's Boeing 707 jets. We landed and took off several times as we conducted meetings throughout his vast territory.

[70] Ibid., p. 1561.

John was always armed with Voice of Prophecy Bible Course enrollment cards. On each flight as soon as we were airborne and it was permissible to unfasten seat belts, John stood, went forward to the cabin, asked the hostess to hand Bible Course enrollment cards to the pilot, copilot, and engineer, tell them to fill in the cards, that he would pick them up before landing. Right and left throughout the length of the cabin, each person received a Bible Course enrollment card, with instructions to quickly fill in name, address, etc. Before landing John gathered the cards.

From stop-to-stop cards properly completed were promptly mailed to the Division Bible School. Brother John repeated this missionary endeavor on each flight. On one flight forty-six persons requested enrollment in the Voice of Prophecy Bible Correspondence Course. Whether traveling by train or plane, he distributed Voice of Prophecy cards which he later carefully processed.

Throughout the world literature evangelists enroll tens of thousands of persons in Bible School courses. They make this a part of their ministry.

Finland's VOP Formula

Finland is a land of enchantment. During winter months it is truly "Winter Wonderland." Pastor Tauno A. Luukanen tells of Finland's Voice of Prophecy work:

For years we have enclosed a Voice of Prophecy Bible Course enrollment card with each of our best selling books. Thus we have enrolled hundreds of Voice of Prophecy students, resulting in scores of new members over the years. Voice of Prophecy enrollment cards used by literature evangelists each have a special mark identifying their

enrollment source. Finland literature evangelists are
notified of souls won by this combined ministry.

In a Little Norwegian Valley,
People Listen With Their Hearts

Student colporteur, T. Sorensen, canvassed in a little
valley in Norway.[71] After selling a doctrinal book to a family,
he inquired regarding the location of the nearest hotel. The
man of the house said, "You would have to back- track a long
way. You are welcome to stay with us." He stayed for three
weeks, selling books throughout the area. Each day he had
worship with the family before departing to his evangelistic
work.

On the last morning of his stay colporteur Sorensen
presented the family one of his message books with the
request, "Read and study the book. Write to me and I will
contact you again."

Come Back

Three years later T. Sorensen received a letter
telling how the man, his wife and neighbors had studied the
book. They invited him to come back. He took with him
Pastor Frenning, director of the Voice of Prophecy Bible
Correspondence School.

The first night back at this home they had a Bible
study. The family enrolled in Norway's Voice of Prophecy
Bible Correspondence School course.

As a result of this combined literature evangelist-
ministerial effort, the father, his wife, three children and three
neighbors were baptized in Lillehammer, Norway.   This

[71]Story by Olav Frenning

is another example of the role of the literature evangelist in world evangelism, leading the way and supporting conference Bible Correspondence Schools. Added to the church in Norway were eight souls who for life would lend strength to Norway and to the world church. Because of the visit of one literature evangelist, there is a church family in this little Norwegian valley.

No More to do With the Pope

A Norwegian literature evangelist visited a lady who loved to read.[72] She purchased a doctrinal volume, enrolled in the Norwegian Voice of Prophecy Bible Correspondence Course, and soon was baptized in Oslo, Norway.

When Olav Frenning visited this newly baptized member she told him how anxious she was for her sister to learn about her new faith. She said, "I have written her and told her about the change of the Sabbath." The sister responded by saying, "If it is true that the Pope changed the Sabbath, I will not have anything more to do with the Pope."

The lady asked if she could enroll her sister in the Bible Correspondence School. "Yes, you must do that," said Olav Frenning. "Let us do it at once!" the lady said. Soon Olav went with the lady to visit the sister, who was later baptized in the Oslo church.

The sisters, anxious for their mother to hear the message, invited her to join them for a visit to a friend's house on Sabbath. There she met an older lady who taught a Sabbath School class. The mother was greatly impressed with this lady's kindness and knowledge of the Scriptures.

The plan was effective. When the mother became a Seventh-day Adventist she said, "I have a Pentecostal friend.

[72] Story by Olav Frenning, Director Norwegian Voice of Prophecy Bible Correspondence School.

I will go and talk to her about this wonderful truth."

From a single literature evangelist contact a lady was won to the church. She won her sister. The sisters won their mother. Mother began working to win a friend. God knew what He was doing when He "ordained the canvassing work," a plan which not only distributes gospel literature but also supports the Bible Correspondence program worldwide. In Norway, as in other areas of the world, a high percentage of faithful Seventh-day Adventists trace their Adventist heritage to the visit of a literature evangelist, the purchase of a message-filled book, and the invitation and completion of a Bible Correspondence School course. God is a Master in soul-winning.

A Study in Mathematics

Though a sale may or may not be made when a literature evangelist visits a home, he/she offers prayer and invites each stranger to enroll in a Bible Course. Literature evangelists are encouraged to enroll as many individuals as possible in a Bible Correspondence Course each week. In 1984 there were 1,840 part-time and full-time licensed and credentialed literature evangelists in the North American Division. A bit of multiplication provides a picture of the evangelistic value of this ongoing ministry.

With interest awakened to matters eternal, strangers begin to find answers to life's questions and are inclined to seriously pursue a Bible study course. A percentage of these persons become supportive members of the Seventh-day Adventist Church.

A Glimpse of Evangelism

The North American Division combined 1984/85 missionary report provides insight into the evangelistic mission of literature evangelists who, in addition to selling millions of dollars worth of doctrine-filled books and journals, additionally engage in a vast missionary endeavor:

> 3,101,000 pieces of literature given
> 309,135 Bible Course enrollments
> 31,736 non-SDAs invited to SDA church services
> 23,202 former SDAs contacted
> 713,332 prayers offered in homes of strangers
> 97,385 Bible studies given
> 4,421 persons baptized

Chapter 7 -
The "Question-and-Answer" Bible

Search Ends in Old Book Store

"Now what is it you are looking for, young fellow?" the old man asked, as he unlocked the door to his dusty bookstore.

"I'm looking for a Bible in question-and-answer form. I know there is one, for I read one at the military base library in Wyoming, but I can't find another like it."

"Hmmmm," the old man thought for a long moment. "Maybe I can help you. Come with me."

It was thus at an old bookstore on the north side of Chicago that airman Jack Blanco, found the "Bible" he had been looking for. He was overjoyed to find it was identical to the one he had read in the Cheyenne library, which had meant so much to him and brought Jesus close to him.[73] It was sometime later when he found that his "Bible" was really the book entitled, *Bible Readings for the Home Circle*, which someone had rebound and entitled "Bible".

While stationed on Guam Jack and another young airman began seriously studying the Bible. Jack was convicted of the seventh-day Sabbath, and decided to simply follow the Lord and keep His commandments, even if he were the only one in the world doing it. When he asked for Sabbath off he was told that the Air Force recognized Sunday as the Lord's Day, not Saturday. Jack explained his convictions to the commanding officer, a pleasant fellow, who turned to the previous officer and said, "If this man wants his Sabbath off, let him have it. He must make his

---

[73]Jolena Taylor King, Jack, an Incredible Life, p. 95.

own arrangements in switching shifts with others, but as long as he does that, then he can go to church if he wants to."[74]

After this Jack decided he was no longer a good Catholic, but didn't know which church to attend. His airman friend, Carl Pinterich, told him there was a church on Guam that kept the seventh day. He invited Jack to go to church with him where Jack met evangelist Ray Turner and mission president Robert Dunton. Friend Carl, who had decided to be baptized before leaving Guam, invited Jack to join him in baptism. When Jack was questioned regarding his beliefs the evangelist found that the Holy Spirit had already led him into believing everything Seventh-day Adventists teach. That Sabbath afternoon baptism at the base of Suicide Cliff (where so many Japanese had died for their country by jumping off rather than surrender) was a fitting symbol of the young airmen's commitment to their Lord.

Who is Jack Blanco?

Dr. Jack Blanco, educator, missionary, author, The Clear Word.

Now retired, Jack Blanco has served as Dean of the School of Religion at Southern Adventist University for a number of years. Since his baptism fifty-nine years ago on the island of Guam he has worked in various church ministries for over forty years.

The author first met Jack just after his baptism when publishing meetings were being held on Guam.

Try to envision the surprise that awaits the literature evangelist who first sold the "Bible" that

Jack found which started him on his forty-year missionary journey, largely devoted to Christian education.

Hogs and Tobacco Have to Go

David and Mandy Mae Walters moved with their family from Jonesboro, Tennessee, to Halfway, Oregon, in the summer of 1921. They bought a house, and in this house they found a copy of a book, *Bible Readings for the Home Circle*. They enjoyed this book and seriously studied it.

Ninety days after moving to Oregon, the family decided to return to Tennessee. One of the things they took back with them was the *Bible Readings* book.

Sometime after returning to Jonesboro, they saw a poster featuring the metal man of Daniel 2, announcing a meeting. Their book told about the "metal man." As a family they decided to attend the meetings. When the meetings ended, the mother and father with three of the older children were baptized. Their lifestyle completely changed: no more hogs, no more tobacco, no more work on Saturday. Friends and neighbors were sure the family would starve; however they determined to trust the Lord, and He prospered them.

Many of the Walters children, grandchildren, and great-grandchildren to the fourth generation are members of the Seventh-day Adventist Church, giving their service, their tithes and offerings.

Ralph Walters, the third son of David and Mandy Mae, still has the copy of *Bible Readings* found in the house in Oregon. His four sons graduated from Seventh-day Adventist schools, and have worked for the church at home and overseas. [75]

[75] Story furnished by Burniece Goetz Walters, 2002.

You can visualize God's light each day, and send it to someone who needs help. Your divine nature must reach out and touch the divine nature of another. Within you is the light of the world; it must be shared with the world.

•Unknown

Found in a Garbage Can

A family in Fort Worth, Texas had a copy of *Bible Readings* which they decided not to keep and threw into their garbage can. The next door neighbor lady found the attractive, beautifully bound, marble-edged book in the garbage can, retrieved it, and began to read. As she studied, she was impressed with its teachings, and searched for a church that worshiped on the seventh-day Sabbath. As a result of her search she became a member of the Ft. Worth Seventh-day Adventist Church.

In heaven this lady will have opportunity to thank an unknown literature evangelist who sold the book which she found in her neighbor's garbage can.

Left on a Back Porch

When Cyril Miller's mother, ill with newly discovered tuberculosis, was searching for truth and a recognition of God's will for her life and for her three small children, she heard a knock at her back door and answered it, only to discover no one there.[76] Looking down on the porch, she saw an old book with a note attached: "Read it and then think." The book was a well-worn copy of *Bible Readings*.

---

[76] Story by Cyril Miller, Vice President, North American Division, letter dated April, 2002.

As she read the book and came to the section on the change of the Sabbath she questioned whether or not this could be true, so she went to the local Catholic priest. He confirmed that it was so.

The mother and children started keeping the Sabbath and later became baptized members of the Seventh-day Adventist church. Today those three children are church workers -- a pastor, a doctor, and a church school teacher.

Launch Out Into the Deep

A ship in the harbor is safe. . . but
that's not what ships were made for.
•Anonymous

Burniece Goetz was canvassing house to house. At the very first home the lady said she was not interested and started to close the door. Quickly Burniece placed in the ladies' hand the pamphlet, "One Hour with Your Bible."

Burniece then went to a house across the street where she met a very interested lady who bought a book. As she was leaving the second home, Burniece saw the first woman sitting out on her porch. The lady called and asked Burniece to return. She had been reading the pamphlet and said, "I have never read anything that makes the Bible so plain." She was now ready to listen and bought a copy of *Bible Readings.*[77]

The ministry of literature evangelists is represented by the angel of Revelation 18:1 who joins his voice with the three angels of Revelation 14 to develop heaven's final cry to the human family. Speaking of the angel of Revelation

---

[77] Story furnished by Burniece Goetz Walters, 2002.

18:1 Ellen White says, "*And in a large degree through our publishing houses is to be accomplished the work of that other angel who comes down from heaven with great power and lightens the earth with his glory.*"[78]

You Were a Long Time Coming

Bruce Borgersen, now a retired pastor, was teaching church school in Glens Falls, New York in the fall of 1967 when the church scheduled an evangelistic series in an air bubble. On a designated Sabbath afternoon church members planned to distribute flyers announcing the meeting. Bruce was assigned a carload of persons, but no one showed up, so he went alone knocking on doors and leaving flyers.

When he rang the bell at one house, there was no response. He rang again and waited. Finally he heard a weak voice saying, "Wait a minute." Soon a seventy-year old lady came to the door. Bruce gave her the flyer and told her about the meetings. She seemed interested but said, "I have no transportation." Bruce suggested that he and his wife would take her to the meetings. She then told him the following story:

When she was sixteen years old, a colporteur sold a copy of *Bible Readings* to her mother. For years they didn't read it. After her parents died, she became interested in the book, and studied it carefully. The flyer advertising the evangelistic meetings reminded her of the message in the book purchased fifty-four years ago.

Hazel Gordon, for this was the elderly woman's name, attended the first meeting with the Borgersens. On the way home she said, "This is what I have been waiting to hear for fifty-four years." She attended each meeting and was baptized. Burdened to tell others what the Lord would do for

[78] Testimonies, Vol. 7, p. 140.

them, she became a colporteur.[79]

> *"It is true that some who buy the books will lay them on the shelf or place them on the parlor table and seldom look at them. Still God has a care for His truth, and the time will come when these books will be sought for and read."*[80]

Bible Readings, topically arranged in question-and-answer form, has special appeal to clergyman because of its organized sermon material. Literature evangelists have circulated *Bible Readings, Daniel and the Revelation,* and *The Great Controversy* across the North American Division like the leaves of autumn. Literature evangelists make millions of initial contacts, which by dedicated follow-up efforts could accelerate the harvest and result in multiple thousands accepting the message of the Three Angels. Names and locations of these thousands of interested persons are available in publishing records for conferences and members interested in doing follow-up work.

> *"Our publications are now sowing the gospel seed, and are instrumental in bringing as many souls to Christ as the preached word. Whole churches have been raised up as the result of their circulation."*[81]

"So Why Shouldn't We Preach the Sabbath?"

The Indianapolis Star, August 25, 2001, reported the following:

> If you hear tambourines or shouts of praise today at Serenity Tabernacle of Faith or Greater New Jerusalem Temple of Truth, it's because they are having church on Saturday.
>
> Pastor of the New Jerusalem church, Herman

---

[79]Letter to the author from Bruce Borgersen, September, 2000.
[80]Testimonies, Vol. 6, pp. 313, 314. (1900), C.M., p. 150.
[81] Review and Herald, June 10, 1880.

H. Davis, said he began searching the scriptures
about a year ago, then learned more in a book called
Daniel and the Revelation, which helped explain the
two Biblical books. "I learned that to have the seal
of God is to observe the Sabbath in its original form,"
the 43-year-old pastor says. "We encourage people to
search the scriptures for themselves."

Pastor R. J. Anthony says a few people
haven't been to the Serenity Tabernacle in awhile. . .
Still he is committed to Saturday worship. "If I don't
preach the truth, I will go to hell – and I ain't going to
hell for nobody!" the 56-year-old pastor says. "God
rested on the seventh day and Jesus rose on the first
day – he even kept the Sabbath in death. So why
shouldn't we keep the Sabbath?"[82]

Searching for Answers

The author is in agreement that though western man is
surrounded by unprecedented luxuries, he is deeply troubled,
uncertain, and uncomfortable regarding life and the future.
Though protected by security locks, side arms, insurance
policies, vicious guard dogs, sentry lighting, and surveillance
cameras, he is experiencing a "many dimensional" illness.
He longs for answers to life's questions:

How did the world originate?

Where is the world bound?

What happens to a man when he dies?

Will there ever be an end to war?

Is there something better in the future?

[82] Reported in Indianapolis Star, August 25, 2001.

Words are inadequate to express the joy a literature evangelist experiences when during a brief visit he observes the light of hope flash across a darkened mind and conviction stir a soul. When a customer is convinced of a literature evangelist's sincerity and realizes that the book being demonstrated will lead him to his Bible for answers, his response will be positive.

On occasion busy persons are hesitant to admit literature evangelists into their homes. However after the sale has been made, it is not unusual for a person to apologize, saying, "At first I thought you were a salesman." The Holy Spirit is at work. Selling, rather than giving literature away, provides serious engagement of thought, important in soul winning.

The literature evangelist is a minister, educator and indeed a salesman. Even when a sales effort seems to have failed, the literature evangelist, ready to depart, will say, "Inasmuch as my work is of a spiritual nature I usually suggest having a brief prayer before I leave. Mr./Mrs. _____, would you mind if, just as we are seated, I offer a brief prayer?" With rare exception permission is granted. One mother said, "Wait to pray until I call the children in." After prayer, though no sale seems evident, the question may be, "What did you say the price is?"

Chapter 8 – Never Too Cold

In telling how his family first connected with Seventh-day Adventists, Elder R. C. (Bob) Mills states, "The weather in Itasca, Wisconsin can be frigid in wintertime. Temperatures may reach 73 degrees below zero. Seventy-seven years ago literature evangelist Joe Levins, canvassing on a cold day, kicked the snow off his heavy boots before entering the Mills home. He had with him the book, *Heralds of the Morning* by O. H. Tait. He showed the book to Jennie Mills, my mother. She purchased the book; the family read it. Our family of four attended an evangelistic meeting and became baptized members of the Seventh-day Adventist Church."

R. C. Mills

Elder Mills still has that book, which he considers a true friend and a treasured possession. Printed on the flyleaf is the following notation: *"This book was the primary agent in bringing Albert and Jennie Mills into the Seventh-day Adventist Church. Attendance at an evangelistic meeting together with the work of a dedicated Bible worker sealed the decision, and the little family of four became members of the Seventh-day Adventist Church."* [83]

The two children, Helen and Robert, were educated in Seventh-day Adventist schools. Helen became a skilled concert pianist.

In various leadership positions Robert Mills worked forty-two years for the Seventh-day Adventist Church, serving both at home and abroad. During these years his musical talents as well as those of his wife, sons, and

[83]Information provided by Elder R. C. Mills, 2001.

daughter have blessed church and campmeeting audiences
around the world.

Elder Mills says theirs was a contribution of service
rather than of finance. However, when added up, their tithes
and offerings over the past seventy-five years amount to a
considerable sum.

Fifty Years Ago in Korea -- Stopped by Military Police

One day in Korea one of our colporteurs
happened upon the scene of a traffic accident. A
child had been hurt so Brother Chong rushed over,
picked up the little child and started off in search of
medical help. He was soon stopped and questioned
by a military policeman. Not sure of Brother Chong's
intentions the police took him and the child to the
military barracks, where the child was given medical
help and Brother Chong was put in prison.

When Brother Chong established his
identity and made clear he was trying to help, the
commanding officer called him into his office for an
interview. This was the opportunity he was waiting
for. He gave the officer a canvass for the *Signs of
the Times*. The officer was favorably impressed and
bought several copies of Signs for himself and family.
He also purchased a supply for each of his men in the
entire military police barracks.

Sometimes the Lord takes us by the collar and
leads us to places where we can do His service![84]

In heaven literature evangelists will hear a chorus of
voices saying, "It was you who invited me here." There will

[84] Reported by C. A. Williams, Publishing Director, Korean Union in the 1950s.

be no regrets for leaving comfortable secular employment to "go search for the lost."

Noise on the Front Lines

When the author visited Korea during wartime in the 1950s conducting institutes, he learned that our colporteurs were going everywhere, even north of the 38th parallel. Colporteur Kim Hung In reported the following:

Sometime ago while canvassing in an area north of Seoul, I made contact with officers of the ROK army. I learned there were 800,000 ROK soldiers on the front lines and in camps just to its rear. I felt impressed that our literature should go to these men. I approached military authorities for permission to go to a village not far from where truce talks were being held. Permission was granted immediately. It actually came in the form of a request to take the Korean Signs of the Times to the ROK forces on the front lines.

I believe I felt as Jonah must have when he received the commission to go to the wicked city of Nineveh to warn the inhabitants of coming judgments. I was aware of the dangers on the front lines. Permission had come easier than expected. I knew I must go.

Publishing Leaders—Korea, standing beside U. S. Army surplus jeep—1953.

When I reached Kim-chon I found the village

to be one large army camp. I began approaching everyone I could with the Korean Signs. In a short time I sold over 300 Signs to the men in this camp.

Even the Ground Shook

Kim Hung In says that, "After leaving this village I went to Tong-Doo-Chon, a point within range of the enemy artillery. The roar of artillery fire from both sides made canvassing difficult. At times the ground would shake. I had to fairly shout to give my canvass."[85]

Cold Most of the Time

Again colporteur Kim Hung In tells of his work:
  I travel most of the time on foot with my books on my back, catching a ride whenever I can. Sometimes I ride in empty boxcars, on top of loaded cars, or in the back of trucks. In the winter I am cold most of the time, but I don't mind when I think of what my Master suffered for me.

Korean Union Literature Evangelists—1952.

[85] Story by Colporteur Kim Hung In.

Literature to Men in Fox Holes

During this last year I sold nearly 4,000 copies
of the Korean Signs of the Times. More than half of
these were sold to young men on the front lines of
battle. I think of these men in their foxholes reading
about the wonderful love of Jesus, and about a land
where there will be no more war, sorrow nor crying.
Then I think that perhaps before he died some Korean
soldier silently and alone gave his heart to God as
a result of reading the Signs or the Marked Bible.
All my suffering from cold, fatigue and sometimes
hunger are as nothing compared with the joy of
having brought salvation to even one of these souls.
Please remember in your prayers these young men on
the front lines.[86]

Hidden Treasures

During the police action in Korea, North Korean
soldiers temporarily overran the Shi Jo Sa Korean Publishing
House. When publishing house employees realized that the
publishing house was certain to be occupied by enemy forces,
printing equipment was disassembled and divided among
employees to be taken to their homes. There each piece was
carefully buried.

As soon as South Korea was again militarily secured,
the buried treasure was unearthed and reassembled. The
writer received the first page run off the reassembled printing
press.

Great Controversy Arm Bands

In a surprise attack Allied troops drove back the
North Korean army. Their departure was so rapid that they

[86]Story by Colporteur Kim Hung In.

left behind a large amount of money. Most interesting was the discovery that from bound copies of the book, *The Great Controversy,* the back bands, bearing the words <u>The Great Controversy,</u> had been removed for use as armbands on North Korean soldiers' uniforms.

I Felt Humbled When I Shook His Hand

During the Korean police action the author was provided a U. S. Army military railroad pass. This made it possible to meet with Korean literature evangelists during wartime. They are surely among the bravest of the brave. One literature evangelist I met had fled the north, sleeping under floors in abandoned homes, hiding in trees and traveling at night when possible. His only clothing was his long winter underwear! I felt humbled when I shook his hand.

Though termed "police action" it was war, real war. I visited a front-line mobile hospital where soldiers with head, chest and abdominal injuries were brought by helicopter. I saw railway refrigerator cars loaded with bodies of young soldiers enroute to the Pusan United Nations cemetery. It has been estimated that one billion soldiers died on earth's battlefields in the century recently ended.

Mary Makoni – Modern Day Martyr

When the author was in South Africa he observed that no nation on earth is exempt from war and cruelty, and was told the following story: Near Johannesburg, South Africa, in a settlement of Alexandra lived Mary Makoni, a champion literature evangelist. During twenty-two years as a literature evangelist she won many souls.

Early in 1986 Mary requested retirement. Two weeks later a group of young people arrived at her home. They asked her to open the door. At first she refused, but they were persistent. Eventually she was convinced that they wanted to pray with her.

When she opened the door they grabbed her and dragged her into the street. A car tire was forced over her shoulders, gasoline was poured over her, and she was set afire.

Neighbors and friends quick to come to Mary's rescue were unable to save her. Mary died the next day.

From her literature ministry she knew many people. I was told that thousands attended her funeral. A modern day martyr, Mary's Christian dedication inspired many to greater service for Christ. As a memorial to Mary literature evangelists of South Africa's Southern Union planned to secure a van which would bear Mary's name, and enter remote areas carrying the gospel.

Chapter 9 -
Like the Leaves of Autumn

"I am living proof that our books should be 'scattered like the leaves of autumn'", said Delora Baggett as she clasped the worn copy of *Bible Readings for the Home Circle* that her grandfather had purchased from a colporteur in 1914. Delora, a literature evangelist from the Gulf States Conference in the Southern Union told her experience while meeting with one hundred other literature evangelists at Daytona Beach in Florida.

Delora related that the *Bible Readings* was given to her father, who kept it for years without reading it. One day when Delora was fourteen years of age, she found the *Bible Readings* tucked away in bookshelves. She took it out, read it, was converted and later joined the Seventh-day Adventist church.

Reports from the convention indicated that the literature evangelists of the Southern Union were indeed scattering books "like the leaves of autumn." During that year (1999) total sales had been over three and one-half million dollars. Fifty-seven persons had been baptized as a result of literature evangelist contacts, 13,721 people enrolled in Bible courses, 548 former Adventists* contacted, and 2,141 Bible studies given.[87]

There are more literature evangelists in the world today than at any time in church history. As the end draws near more articles and books will be written telling of God's continuing blessings upon house-to-house evangelism.

---

*There are an estimated 1,000,000 former Seventh-day Adventists in North America.
[87] Southern Tidings, March 1999, p. 17.

At the Turn of the Century
"May I Sleep in Your Barn Tonight Mister?"

During early days of Seventh-day Adventist publishing ministry literature evangelists were often away from home and family weeks at a time, sometime even months, staying with the people on their farms, and helping with evening chores before joining the family for supper and evening. After supper the family would gather around the large kitchen table, and with a kerosene lamp turned high enough for all to see, they opened the Scriptures, and the literature evangelist would explain how the books helped people understand the Bible.

Tuberculosis Was a Killer

During the latter part of the nineteenth century tuberculosis was a major killer in the United States. It was also a time when surgeons wore their street clothes when performing an operation and carried their instruments in a bag as they went from one patient's home to another.

Around the time of the turn of the twentieth century, hydrotherapy was a popular method of treatment at Seventh-day Adventist health centers. Many lay persons knew the benefits of hydrotherapy and were able to give these treatments.

Visit to the Schaeffer Farm

In 1919 a now unknown literature evangelist called at the farm home of a German family in Pennsylvania, unaware that the doctor had just departed, giving no hope that the father would survive the ravages of the flu epidemic. The doctor's sad words were, "There is nothing more I can do for him."

When the literature evangelist learned of the father's serious condition, he asked if he could be of help. "I can give hydrotherapy treatments with hot and cold water," he said. The desperate family was ready for any kind of help, even hot and cold water treatments from a stranger!

Hydrotherapy treatments were begun immediately, and soon the father's temperature began to lower. The family was overjoyed with a glimmer of hope that he was on his way to recovery. Had the literature evangelist not visited that home, the father might not have survived.

This literature evangelist returned and gave Bible studies to the Schaeffer family. The parents believed what they heard and became baptized members of the Seventh-day Adventist Church.

Six years went by. Another son, Russell, was born to the family. Russell says, "God was leading in my life from the very beginning. I had many happy days growing up on the farm."

Influence of a Bible Teacher

Russell attended public schools for the first ten grades, and then a Bible teacher from Shenandoah Valley Academy in Virginia visited Pennsylvania. Because of this teacher's influence the parents agreed that Russell should attend Shenandoah Valley Academy for his junior and senior high school years. Though very homesick,

Russell Schaeffer

he didn't give up. During those two years Russell decided to enter the Lord's work in some special way.

For forty years Professor Russell Schaeffer taught in the Seventh-day Adventist church school system. His two sons, ninth-generation Schaeffers in America, and third-generation Seventh-day Adventists, attended Seventh-day Adventist schools from first grade through university. Both are leaders in local churches. Russell says, "When I get to heaven, I want to meet and thank that literature evangelist who rescued my father from certain death, and who brought the message of everlasting hope to our family."[88]

Fleming Plaza
Cora's Visit to Relatives

Young Cora Chase was always pleased to have opportunity to visit with her aunts and grandmothers. They were such fun. One particular day, well over one hundred years ago, Cora was at the home of one of the aunts in central Wisconsin when a knock came at the door. A colporteur (literature evangelist) introduced himself, saying he was making Christian calls in the community. Neither aunts nor grandmothers belonged to any church, nor did they seem inclined in that direction. However, finally one grandmother bought the book, *Bible Readings for the Home Circle.*

As a group they decided to meet one day each week and read from the book for an hour or two. This they did until they came to such verses as Genesis 2:2, 3 and Exodus 20:8-11 regarding the seventh day Sabbath. That was too much. They decided to abandon their study and forget about it.

That is, all except Cora. She couldn't forget what they had read from the Scriptures and from the book. The

[88]Schaeffer story furnished to author by Russell Schaeffer, September 2000.

information from the book remained with her through her growing up years.

Finally Cora met and married Charles Fleming. They were living in Oshkosh, Wisconsin, when she heard of a church in that city that worshipped on the seventh day. She decided to visit this church, which she did several times. Cora was convinced of the truth that she had discovered years before in the book sold by a gospel salesman. When Cora told her husband of her conviction, he pledged his support.

Two children were added to the family, Charles E. Fleming, Jr., and a young sister. About that time the Flemings moved to north central Wisconsin, where they owned and operated a Ford car agency.  Unfortunately for the young mother and her children, there was not another Seventh-day Adventist in the whole county where they lived. How was she going to successfully raise her children in harmony with the teachings of the book? She subscribed to *My Little Friend* and *The Youth's Instructor*. Her children were taught to honor God, to keep the Sabbath, and live Christian lives. Though

Charles E. Fleming, Jr

far removed from Seventh-day Adventist schools, when the time came for higher education, both Charles and his sister attended Emmanuel Missionary College in Michigan [now Andrews University].[89]

Charles (Chick) Fleming, Jr. spent his working years serving his church, first at Forest Lake Academy in Florida, later as Treasurer of the Georgia-Cumberland Conference, and then for thirty years as Business Manager of Southern Adventist College [now University]. His Christian and business influence had much to do with the development of the spiritual and economic stability of Southern Adventist

---

[89] Story provided to author in letter from Charles Fleming, February 2000.

University. The Collegedale shopping area across from
the University is named Fleming Plaza. The following
inscription with Charles Fleming's face in bronze appears on
the outer wall of the United States Post Office in Collegedale,
Tennessee.

**Fleming Plaza is dedicated in honor
of Charles "Chick" Fleming, Jr., a Christian
gentleman.**

**His business sense, ethical principles
and faith in action as General Manager
for Finance and Development from 1946-
1975 cultivated phenomenal growth of the
college enrollment, work opportunities and
physical plant.**

Dedicated May 4, 1986.

This story of literature evangelism provided to
the author by Charles Fleming, Jr. portrays a mother's
commitment to God, to her children and to Christian
education.

Tribe Versus Tribe

During the eighteenth century, when the British were
colonizing West Africa making treaties with various tribes in
Nigeria, they invited tribal chiefs to allow them to educate
their sons; the chiefs were skeptical, so gave them their Ibo
servant boys.

In subsequent years as the Ibo tribesmen became the
educated; they operated civil services throughout Nigeria,
they owned houses and businesses and drove cars, were
aggressive and successful, and became the driving power

of the nation. Wherever literature evangelist sales training seminars were conducted in Nigeria, the majority of students were young people from the Ibo tribe.

The Hausa tribe, less educated at the time, had to depend on trained Ibo tribesmen to operate the government. Over time bad feelings developed into violent fighting between tribes. Words are not adequate to describe the bitterness that resulted. The most difficult experience for a native was to belong to the wrong tribe.

East Africa Literature Evangelists, 1973. They represent Africa's hundreds of energetic literature evangelists. For decades literature evangelists have planted gospel seed throughout Africa in preparation for the final harvest.

During the uprising in 1967 the author stayed in the home of an American missionary. Before my arrival, houses, businesses, cars, and earthly possessions of Ibo tribesmen had been confiscated; they became hunted and hated. A time had been secretly appointed throughout the nation to slay the Ibos. At that time, out of loyalty, a Hausa servant boy would slay his fellow Ibo servant boy. A few nights before, seven Ibos had been murdered outside the bedroom window of the room where I slept. There had been a house-to-house search for Ibos. When found, they were stripped of their clothing and destroyed.

In the pastor's house, located a short distance from the road, was a frightened Ibo servant lad. Quickly, before the searchers arrived, drawer bottoms were removed from a chest of drawers so the Ibo lad could hide. As the house was searched understandably the frightened boy was deathly quiet. During the hours of darkness, the young man was placed in the trunk of the pastor's car and taken to safety.

"Your Book Has Saved Your Life"

Paul Chima
(Photo by Paul Sundquist)

During this troubled time with tensions high one of our brave Ibo literature evangelists was traveling in a taxi with passengers of other tribes. An army officer with his soldiers stopped the taxi. The officer asked, "Are there any Ibos in here?" All eyes focused on the Ibo man with the briefcase, in which was one book he had been unable to deliver.

The Ibo was dragged from the taxi. Before stripping him of clothes prior to plans to destroy him, the officer demanded, "What is in the briefcase?"

"A book," answered the literature evangelist.

"Take it out!" demanded the officer.

Holding the book upside down to himself, as he had been taught, the literature evangelist nervously endeavored to reveal the message of the book, entitled, *God's Answers*. "Sir," he said, "This book holds the answer to Nigeria's problems."

The officer was so impressed that he stopped the next taxi, paid the fare, and said as he pushed the Ibo bookman into the taxi, "Flee for your life. Your book has saved your life!"[90]

[90]Story furnished by Paul Chima.

Attempts at ethnic cleansing are not new to mankind. World War II is a major example. History is replete with man's inhumanity to man. Jesus, only Jesus, is the solution.

One wonders if today's evangelists who conduct large meetings overseas and report great numbers baptized understand the bravery of literature evangelists who courageously created a pathway for them. How aware are they of church world history?

Champion Blind Bowler Becomes Champion Colporteur

Irene Denny Larkin Mitchell tells the story of her blind colporteur uncle:

Victor Roy Foskett, born with poor eyesight, became totally blind in his late twenties. Roy's special interest was bowling. When he became blind he signed on with a trainer to become a professional blind bowler and in 1939 was the Champion Blind Bowler of America.

One day the Fosketts found an advertisement at their door announcing evangelistic meetings. Thrilled with the message they were soon baptized. Roy felt he could no longer continue bowling, as in those days nearly all bowling alleys were in taverns.

Roy Foskett, a blind Literature Evangelist, standing by one month's supply of *Life & Health* and *These Times* magazines.

It became necessary for Roy to seek other employment. For a time he worked in a broom factory and then in a baby buggy factory. However, he felt convicted that he should be working for the Lord, and decided to sell *Life and Health* and *These Times* magazines in business districts of the city. He took two vacations to give it a try. The Lord blessed him. He did so well he continued selling magazines until his death, often leading in sales in the Missouri Conference.

Roy Foskett's ability as a blind person to make his way around the city of St. Louis, visiting places of business, was a special accomplishment. He gave honor and glory to the Lord for watching over him.

Two Christian business partners, who purchased magazines from Roy, sold a strategically located piece of property to a group of Seventh-day Adventists as a place to build a church, however, they vowed to never join the Seventh-day Adventist Church.

One day these men found a Bible Correspondence Course advertised in *These Times* magazine. They signed up for the course, and became curious to know what religious denomination sponsored the lessons. The address listed on the lessons was Kansas City, Missouri. To their amazement when they arrived at the address in Kansas City it was the headquarters office of the Missouri Conference of Seventh-day Adventists! Upon returning to St. Louis, they began attending the Southside Seventh-day Adventist Church and were soon baptized.

We will not know this side of heaven the far-reaching effects of the witness of one blind literature evangelist - Victor Roy Foskett. After traveling a great distance down the highway of life in darkness he now sleeps awaiting the day when he will not only hear voices but actually see the faces of trophies of his earthly labors.[91]

---

[91] Story by Irene Denny Larkin Mitchell, niece of Victor Roy Foskett.

Quadrennial Soul-Winning Report[92]

At the 1954 General Conference Session in San Francisco, California, the following evangelistic achievements were reported:

One Hundred Twenty-Five

During his literature evangelist ministry, R. J. Jones of Minnesota has personally won one hundred twenty-five souls to the message . He feels that his efforts are successful when men and women accept Christ because of his commitment.

100 Souls Won in Houston

Brother and Sister M. L. Tidwell of Houston have distributed more than $100,000.00 worth of books and magazines during the ten years prior to 1954. They worked closely with ministers in their territory and won one hundred souls to the truth.

Two Churches – 150 Souls

Mrs. C. J. Cain, of the Lake Region Conference worked for ten years as a literature evangelist. Her deliveries averaged $6,000.00 of *Bible Readings* annually. God rewarded her faithfulness by more than 150 souls baptized into the truth, and two churches being raised up.

Mrs. C. J. Cain

[92] The Publishing Department Story Quadrennial Report, presented at the 47th session of the General Conference of Seventh-day Adventists in San Francisco, 1954.

"A Walk Around the World"

Glen Shelton of Iowa was an active colporteur for forty-six years. During that time he not only brought ninety-four persons into church fellowship, he also walked the distance equivalent to a walk around the world.

Primitive Methodists Become Adventist Leaders

In 1906 there were no Seventh-day Adventists in the beautiful south coast town of Bournemouth, England, that is until literature evangelist John Jeremiah Green called at the home of a young twenty-one year old hydraulic engineer. This happily married man and his wife were Primitive Methodists. At age seventeen he had begun service as a lay preacher but never had he been able to control his knocking knees and pounding heart whenever he entered the pulpit. Nor had he been able to conquer the smoking habit. Even drink figured in his "weaknesses" on festive occasions.

Literature Evangelists, British Union—1966

The book this young man bought, *Our Paradise Home* by S. H. Lane, originally published by the Review and Herald Publishing Association, had almost instantaneous results. With the added help of personal Bible studies with literature evangelist Green he accepted the cardinal truths of the Adventist faith within six weeks of purchase. A week later his wife joined him as a Sabbath keeper. A few more weeks and he had prevailed on his married sister to join the ranks of Sabbath keepers.

Another book which permanently stabilized the young man and his family in the faith was *The Great Controversy*.

Desiring to share his faith more effectively, the young man abandoned his engineering and even though not yet baptized, joined John Jeremiah Green in the literature ministry.

So also did his wife in an unusual way. It was publishing house practice in those days to use back numbers of *Present Truth* as packing in crates of bound books. The best of these she carefully ironed flat and then distributed. Within months she won a married couple to the Adventist faith who, after some years in private business, located on Stanborough Park, Watford, where they installed and operated the Sanitarium laundry.

A. M. Vine, this young man who became an Adventist and then a literature evangelist, was not a high-pressure salesman. However, his years in the literature ministry prepared him for over forty years service as elder and preacher in Bournemouth and other places in England. Though never noted for its material affluence, his home was a happy Christian home. He provided his sons and daughter with books that fired their imagination with the importance and thrill of missionary service.

The three sons, A. C. Vine, R. D. Vine and K. L. Vine all became ordained ministers in the Seventh-day Adventist church. Later three grandsons, A. M. Vine, R. L. Vine, and R. G. Vine also joined the ministerial ranks of the Adventist church.[93]

[93] Related in 1967 by second son, R. D. Vine, editor, Stanborough Press Ltd., Grantham, Lincs., England.

Chapter 10 -
You've Got Mail – Lots of Mail

Rent a Church – Start a Meeting

Pastor Cordell E. Reiner, now ministering in Texas, told the author that as a student literature evangelist he learned how to lead persons to make decisions. Early in his ministry Pastor Reiner was asked to go to a city where there was no Seventh-day Adventist church nor an Adventist presence. His conference president told him to rent a church and begin meetings.

He visited the Presbyterian minister in the selected area and inquired if he could rent his church. The minister asked, "How many members do you have here?" "None," Pastor Reiner replied. Perhaps the Presbyterian minister had compassion on the young preacher, for he rented the church for only twenty-five dollars a month.

In preparation for the evangelistic meeting, Pastor Reiner took with him a supply of paid-out literature evangelist customer contract sales records each giving the name, address and telephone number, plus a list of books and journals purchased. He made contact with these persons, who by purchasing our books and journals had given evidence of interest in matters eternal.

As a result of this combined evangelistic effort, seventeen persons were baptized into the Seventh-day Adventist church.[94]

---

[94] Story told to the author by Cordell E. Reiner, July 2001.

120

Student Scholarships – Pastoral Training

The foregoing story indicates that Cordell Reiner received valuable training as a student literature evangelist; that as a student he had learned how to enter homes and unlock human hearts. One hundred years ago the church was given this suggestion: *"Those fitting for the ministry can engage in no other occupation that will give them so large an experience as the canvassing work."*[95]

When a student successfully earns a scholarship by entering into homes of strangers, selling doctrinal decision volumes, making person-to-person gospel sales appeals, gaining decisions, studying the characters of men, he gains a wealth of experience. Whatever vocation this student follows in life, such canvassing achievement will be of great value and will enrich the church.

Five Hundred Responded

In 1993 Lake Union president, Robert Carter, told that when letters were sent to paid-out customers in the Lake Union, five hundred persons responded requesting Bible studies. Evangelist Don Gray said, "These are the best leads we have had."

The term Home Health Education Service [HHES] is used to identify the office that processes cash and credit subscription sales made by literature evangelists to the public. Each customer sales contract provides the name, address and telephone number of the person who purchased the book or journal. The church's Publishing Department offices have records of multiple thousands of paid-out customer names, with relevant data -- a gold mine of potential souls to be made ready for the Kingdom.

[95] Testimonies, Vol. 6, p. 334 (1900).

Evangelistic Follow-up

For evangelistic follow-up, paid-out customer names represent persons who have made a substantial investment in literature featuring the message of the Three Angels. The effort by literature evangelists may rightly be termed, "jump-start evangelism," requiring follow-up attention.

Elder Joe Whedbee, former publishing director of the Ontario, Canada Conference conducted a publishing department follow-up experiment in Windsor, Ontario, calling on one hundred homes of "paid-out" customers. Of the fifty families found at home, eighteen enrolled in Bible studies. *"God does not generally work miracles to advance His truth. If the husbandman neglects to cultivate the soil after sowing the seed, God works no miracle to counteract the sure result of neglect."*[96]

Conferences, "You've Got Mail – Lots of Mail!" Over a century of seed sowing is ready for harvest. Soul-winning opportunities are legion.

MagaBook Program
A Special Nationwide Training for Adventist Youth

Hundreds of students are annually engaged in the 10-Week MagaBook Scholarship Program, one of North America's most worthy, productive, and fast growing person-to-person youth ministries. During the summer of 2001 two hundred thirty dynamic young men and women in North American Division's Southern Union visited an estimated 1,000,000 families, delivering $967,346.00 worth of gospel light. These young people receive first-hand knowledge in human relations and are filled with joyful stories as they return with scholarships to their various schools ready for

---

[96] Adventist Review, September 27, 2001, Ellen G. White.

another term of study. Similarly in other union conference territories publishing directors, as educators, direct this invaluable phase of Christian education, translating classroom theory into reality.

Southern Union Conference Student Literature Evangelists—2001.

Each MagaBook contains two tear-out response cards, one for additional literature and the other an invitation to enroll in the Discover Bible Correspondence Course.

The MagaBook student program is one of the church's most noble evangelistic ministries, empowered by youth, blessed by the Holy Spirit.

Southern Union Full-Time Literature Evangelists Convention—2003

Student Soul Winners

In five years Southern Union student literature evangelists sold and delivered $2,891,416.00 worth of message laden gospel books and journals.

The Southern Union Conference operates a training school located in the Florida Conference for literature evangelists known as S O U L S (Southern Outreach Literature School) where Christian salesmanship theory and field training are taught by skilled publishing department educators. Youth who gain this highly practical training acquire a special understanding of self and humanity – a valuable educational achievement.

The Lead Card Plan – A Door Opener!
Provides Easy Access into Homes of Strangers

The Bible Story Lead Card Plan originated in 1955 with a literature evangelist of the North Pacific Union. The program rapidly spread across the North American Division.

27-201

BUSINESS REPLY MAIL
FIRST CLASS MAIL   PERMIT NO. 78   HAGERSTOWN, MD

POSTAGE WILL BE PAID BY ADDRESSEE

NO POSTAGE
NECESSARY
IF MAILED
IN THE
UNITED STATES

PO BOX 1119
HAGERSTOWN, MD 21741-9923

Bible Story Lead Card with Literature Evangelist Code Number.

Hundreds of thousands of sample copies of Volume 1 of the ten-volume *The Bible Story* set are found in as many professional waiting rooms across the nation. The wide distribution of these sample books is in itself a recommendation for the visit of a literature evangelist. This plan has broad spiritual effect on society and ensures easy entry into homes.

Soul-Winning Display Copies Everywhere

While waiting in the office of an optometrist the
author was seated next to a construction contractor. He asked
what my work was in the real world. Suspended prominently
from an attractive display of eye-glasses was a *Bible Story*
Lead Card holder. I pointed to the Lead Card holder and said
I had much to do with the books advertised, that they were
available in thirteen languages. I mentioned that I knew the
author personally, and was with him during his last overseas
trip.

Hal, the construction contractor, said: "My brother
once studied to be a Nazarene preacher, but he lost his faith.
One day, seated in a doctor's office, he read a story from a
display copy of *The Bible Story*, which reignited his faith
in God." Hal then said, "These display copies seem to be
everywhere!"

Bob Long, recently retired, began attending a
Thursday morning Bible study class in Collegedale,
Tennessee. Formerly he sold pharmaceutical products. He
told that while waiting for opportunity to present his products
to a doctor, he removed a "lead card" from *The Bible Story*
display copy, Volume I. He mailed the card. A literature
evangelist came to his home. He became a Seventh-day
Adventist. In telling this experience to the author he spoke
of the literature evangelist by name – Robert Petry. I knew
this career literature evangelist. Hundreds of people certainly
know him.

Most people in North America have seen and
examined these special books. On the inside cover of each
sample volume is an open-ended envelope which contains
prepaid postage response cards. This card bears a number
identifying the literature evangelist who places and maintains
each sample book in his/her assigned territory. Like a

trapper running his trap line, the literature evangelist is responsible for ensuring an adequate supply of response cards. Thousands of completed cards are continually being mailed to HHES offices. Literature evangelists

Arthur S. Maxwell, most widely read author of children's Bible story and character building books. We traveled together during his last overseas trip.

are notified of interest responses and make contact with prospective customers. In this way millions of dollars worth of the ten-volume Bible Story sets are placed in homes, together with other books such as *The Great Controversy*, *Desire of Ages*, and *Bible Readings*.

It Began in a Doctor's Waiting Room

On the banks of the Delaware River in a quiet little New Jersey town, two families, one Catholic and the other Jewish, lived near each other. These families visited the same family doctor where they found a sample copy of *The Bible Story*. The card in the inside pocket of the book gave them opportunity to indicate their interest. A visit from a literature evangelist followed. Soon each family had its own set of *The Bible Story*.

These books were eagerly read each night until in the course of a year the ten volumes had been completed. Evidently neither of these families had been attending their respective churches, but as the story of the love of Jesus was unfolded in their homes through the pages of *The Bible Story* a desire and need of finding a church home came to both families. They both began attending the Calvary Presbyterian Church near their homes.

When the books were shown to the pastor of this large church his reaction was favorable and immediate. He recognized the books as Seventh-day Adventist books and at the same time realized their wonderful potential. One mother related how her children had enjoyed the stories read to them night after night and how Bible characters like David, Peter and Paul had become more thrilling to them than TV characters. Because of this happy experience in her home she, with the pastor, planned a story hour for the children of their church. A special service was scheduled during the sermon hour. More than fifty wide-eyed children crowded together and eagerly listened as Uncle Arthur's *Bible Stories* were read to them.

This thrilling episode came to the forefront when T. K. Martin, art director at the Review and Herald Publishing Association, received a long-distance telephone call from the New Jersey pastor asking if he could obtain large pictures of the illustrations in the books to show to the children as the stories were being read from week to week.[97]

Does the literature evangelist Lead Card Plan truly work? Indeed it does! The inflow of thousands of lead cards continues, where conferences encourage it.

Jimmy Sleeps with *The Bible Story* Books

Jimmy Nagy, a Cleveland, Ohio boy, was thought to be afflicted with an incurable bone disease. While waiting for the doctor one day, he picked up a copy of the Volume 1 of *The Bible Story*. He liked the book and sent in a response card.

[97] Columbia Union Visitor, December 20, 1962.

When literature evangelist, Claude Diehl, called at the home he found Jimmy and his mother very interested. They purchased a set of *The Bible Story.* Diehl lent the mother a copy of *God Speaks to Modern Man.* On his first call back the mother expressed interest in what she was learning from this book. As for Jimmy, he liked his B*ible Story* books so much he was sleeping with them.

Jimmy Nagy

Soon the mother and son became interested in the message found in the books and were baptized. Later a daughter and her girlfriend joined the church. Before the story ended, Jimmy's brother and his girlfriend were awaiting baptism. Six souls! The result of one lead card found in a doctor's waiting room.[98]

Where are the Cowboys?

Literature evangelist Wayne Welborne, publishing director in the Ohio Conference, told the author about giving a sales demonstration for Uncle Arthur's ten-volume *The Bible Story* set to a mother and son. Little Johnny was captivated by the pictures and stories being presented until the moment the TV repairman arrived. Immediately Johnny hurried to where the repairman was pushing the television away from the wall to gain access to its vital parts. While the repairman was working, Johnny was crowding in for a careful look. Suddenly he backed away, looked up at the repairman, and asked, "Where are the cowboys"?

Night after night Johnny had doubtless watched cowboys being shot off horses or from behind rocks. He went to bed certain that cowboys were dying inside the TV and wondering if any survived.

[98] Reported by Elder Paul Bernet when Publishing Director of Ohio Conference.

Life of Service

The manager of the Georgia-Cumberland Adventist
Book Center in Collegedale, Tennessee, Doug Anderson,
traces his heritage to a literature evangelist. His great
grandmother bought a book from a literature evangelist. The
family joined the Seventh-day Adventist church. Doug,
a fourth generation Seventh-day Adventist, with his life
committed to service for the church he loves, has served
many years in denominational publishing houses and
Adventist Book Centers.

From Executive Secretary to Literature Evangelist

Marie Thomas, a member of the Seventh-day
Adventist church, was a successful executive secretary in
St. Louis, Missouri. A fellow church member told her that
the Lord wanted her in the bookwork. Finally she decided
that with the Lord's help she would become a literature
evangelist. She worked hard. During 1986 Marie sold
over $30,000.00 worth of literature and also conducted two
Revelation Seminars. Fifty-nine people finished the first
Seminar course, and sixteen of these persons were baptized.

Armageddon and Doomsday

"Time as an ever-rolling tide, bears all her sons and
daughters away."[99] God's plan for man is more, much more
than simply one wave of humanity following another over
the face of the earth. Humanity is rounding the final curve of
human history. The Damocles swords of Armageddon and
doomsday are suspended over this generation, a fact which
inspires laymen to become literature evangelists.

[99]From "Winning the Prize" by B. E. Leach, President, Southwestern Union Conference.

Literature evangelists meet earth's sincere persons who live under life's darkening shadows. Their ministry, like the work of the apostle Paul, is tactfully urging strangers to choose life's glorious final destination. This work is accomplished not alone by well chosen words but by the ministry of the Holy Spirit. *"Not by might, nor by power, but by My Spirit, saith the Lord of hosts."*[100]

Growing Up – Seriously!

Oregon's late Democratic Senator Richard Newberger underwent five months of treatment for cancer, including surgery and cobalt radiation. Shortly before returning to Washington to resume his duties in the Senate, he expressed this bit of philosophy:

> *We're all flesh, be it Republican or Democrat, rich banker or poorly paid college professor. I think it would be almost impossible for me to get angry at someone over a political issue. It doesn't make any difference anymore whether my wife squeezes toothpaste from the top or the bottom, if the biscuits are burned or if the living room is cluttered . . . . No one really grows up until he realizes he has to die.* Life is a trust to be lived seriously.

Lord of the Great Controversy

"Signs of the times everywhere" said Dr. Bert B. Beach, Director of Interchurch Relations, General Conference of Seventh-day Adventists. "Seventh-day Adventists have, from their earliest history, seen the Papacy as a major

Dr. B. B. Beach

---

[100] Zechariah 4:6.

actor in the apocalyptic scene of final events. I believe that the fulfillment of eschatological events will be grander and indeed more spectacular than the anticipation of our finite minds. God is not the prisoner of our limited biblical understanding. He is the Creator of history and is the Lord of the great controversy."[101]

"The proclamation of the gospel is the only means in which God can employ human instrumentality for the salvation of souls."[102] *"The earth shall be filled with the knowledge of the glory of the Lord, as the waters cover the sea."*[103]

Ordained Advance Guard

W. R. Beach, former Secretary of the General Conference, and father of Dr. B. B. Beach, made this meaningful statement:
Literature evangelism is ordained of Heaven. It is a fruitful way of winning souls. I know, because it was a literature evangelist who first introduced my parents to God's everlasting truth. At home and around the world, our literature evangelists are the advance guard, preparing the way for others to reap a harvest of souls. They are among our most valued workers.[104]

Missent Colporteur Newsletter

Two men with the same first and surnames were living on the same street in the same block in a town in Louisiana. One was a literature evangelist whose publishing department newsletter with soul-winning experiences was being received and read by his neighbor.

[101] Adventist Review, July 2001.
[102] Seventh-day Adventist Bible Commentary, Vol. 7, p. 984.
[103] Habakkuk 2:14.
[104] E. R. Palmer, The Printing Press and the Gospel, p. 139.

After some weeks the publishing department office received a letter from this neighbor which read, "Recently I have been receiving a bulletin which greatly impresses me. I don't know what the word 'Colporteur' means, but I think I would like to be one."

Time to Talk to the Lord

The following story provides insight into the ministry of one literature evangelist's day of trial:

He was discouraged that morning and didn't want to go out canvassing, but forced himself to drive to his territory.

Secret for Success

By midafternoon having made no sales and not finding people home, it was time to talk to the Lord. He stopped beside the road to pray and read his Bible, which opened to the book of Job. The first three chapters totally changed his attitude. True, he hadn't had a sale for three days, but compared to Job's experiences he really shouldn't worry. After his talk with the Lord he continued on his way with a happy attitude.

Evening came. He had four lead cards left for homes in the area. No one answered at the first three homes. It was 7:00 P. M. when he arrived at the last house, where he found the man working in his yard. Children were outside playing. After being invited inside the literature evangelist presented his canvass to the family. The interest of the parents became evident. As the presentation was concluding, the father looked at their little girl and said, "Rose, if Mom and Dad buy these books will you listen carefully as we read the stories to you?" The little five-year old daughter replied, "Yes, I like these books, Daddy." The father turned to the nine-year old son and asked, "Are you going to read these books?" The son responded, "Yeah, Dad, I'll read them." The father then addressed the fifteen-year old son, "What about you, son? Will you read these books?" The son replied, "Dad, I have access to any kind of reading material. I want to read something that will enlarge my mind." The father turned to the literature evangelist and said, "Well, I guess you have sold these books."[105]

In the sales presentation literature evangelists, like the artist, paint a mental picture of parents with their children, eventual members of heaven's eternal family.

Accurate Reporting

The author was told of a new literature evangelist whose weekly sales report seemed excessive for a beginner. The publishing director, believing he did not understand the reporting procedure, went to visit the new worker. The leader was invited to spend the night with the worker. They slept in the same room.

---

[105] Southern Union Conference Literature Evangelist Newsletter, Nov. 2001.

It was summer time. During the night the leader awakened to discover that he was alone in the room. Through an open window he heard a voice. It was the voice of the missing bookman. Silhouetted in the moonlight, kneeling under a tree, he was making contact with the Designer of life, the God of the Great Controversy.

The leader now understood that the literature evangelist not only knew how to accurately fill out his weekly reports, but that he was in constant contact with the Source of true power. Prayer – heaven's great key! It is the breath of the soul.[106]

For a Moment of Time

It was during the forty-five-year reign of Queen Elizabeth I that England's colonial future began. From this geographically small island empire, England's navy roamed the seven seas in search of new lands and new wealth. During these years the British flag circled the earth. England controlled much of the earth's surface and a major portion of the human family. They opened the door for missionaries and introduced parliamentary procedure to the world.

History records that in spite of this great power, upon her death bed Queen Elizabeth exclaimed, "All my possessions for a moment of time."[107] When a man dies the accumulations of his life instantly become the possession of others. "*His breath goeth forth, he returneth to his earth; in that very day his thoughts perish.*"[108]

Time and life cannot be valued rightly until they are seen in relation to eternity. "Deep calleth unto deep."

---

[106] This story reported to author during his years in publishing ministry.
[107] Oxford Dictionary of Quotations, p. 274 (1992).
[108] Psalms 146:4.

Ships That Pass in the Night

After retirement from the General Conference in 1980, when the author was still living in the Washington, DC area, he was invited to serve as leader of the first North American Division Adventist Retired Workers' Club. We later moved to Collegedale, Tennessee where I served for three years as president of the local Adventist Retired Workers' Club. During ARW gatherings I looked upon the sea of gray heads and bent bodies with awe and respect, realizing that they were faithful builders of world church organizations at home and abroad. Their footsteps are embedded in the soil of every nation. Many with whom I first served are now at rest. They lived and served, leaving quietly one by one, each as a ship traveling down the river of life to the open sea.

Most men and many of the women of this generation were once student literature evangelists. They met mental and physical challenges, translating theory into reality by using the art of reason and persuasion so important in winning souls. They were trained to be thinkers and movers. Such training is important to the church today.

Chapter 11 – Invincible Vikings

Land of the Vikings

The land of Norway, mostly a high plateau, also has a jagged coastline of fjords. One fjord (inlet) extends inland one hundred miles. Including all fjords and peninsulas, the full length of Norway's coastline is approximately 12,500 miles, one-half the distance around the world. Permanent ice/snow covers 1,200 square miles of Norway's uplands. One glacier covers 190 square miles.[109]

Literature evangelist Olar Kolvik was following a lead given him by a teacher/customer, which would take him to a remote settlement of three families. From the point of reference it was a twelve-mile walk one way, or he could travel by car into Sweden and cross a lake to return to Norway. Olar chose the longer route.

When he arrived at the lake with his sets of books, a boatman wanted twenty-five kroner to take Olar across the lake. The price seemed too much, so he hired a rowboat for two kroner and rowed for one and one-half hours to cross the seven miles of lake. It was only a kilometer (4/5 of a mile) walk to the first house, where he sold a ten-volume *The Bible Story* set and was asked to make immediate delivery. Olar walked back to the rowboat where one set of *The Bible Story* was safely waiting.

Olaf Vetna,
Publishing House Manager,
Norway, 1967.

[109] The World Encyclopedia, Vol. 14, p. 418, 1968.

The second family was unable to buy. However, the third family ordered a set of *The Bible Story*. This set was delivered when the man of the house took Olar and his rowboat back to the other side of the lake where, from his car, he delivered another set of books.

By now it was 10:30 p.m., but the Lord blessed the persistence of this Viking. He spent the night in his car and the next day returned to his territory, where he met five Laplander families and sold four sets of *The Bible Story*.[110]

Many Norwegian church members trace their Adventist heritage to the visit of a literature evangelist.

Heaven's Praying Vikings

During the writer's six years in the Northern Europe-West Africa Division (now Trans European Division), it was a privilege to meet annually with the bookman army of each conference or mission throughout the entire division. Among my fondest memories of Norway are the earnest

General Conference President, R. H. Pierson, addresses Tri-Division Publishing Council Delegates—1971.

prayers of the bookmen, which revealed the depth of their concern for people they met in their ministry. I will never forget, for I knew I had been in the presence of heaven's praying Vikings.

"*The Advent Tidende,* a Danish-Norwegian paper, the first non-English periodical published by Seventh-day Adventists, was begun by John G. Matteson who had

---

[110]This experience related during 1968 Literature Evangelist Institute in Norway.

immigrated to America."[111]   Nearly one hundred years ago a
Seventh-day Adventist publishing house was built in Norway.

Whaling Ship For Sale

The young captain of a whaling ship was sailing
in the northern Arctic Sea when his ship narrowly escaped
disaster, after being battered in a severe storm. Captain
Havstein had previously taken life for granted but his narrow
escape with death in icy waters caused him to think seriously.

Tre-divisionskongressen i Jönköping
TREHUNDRA DELEGATER DISKUTERADE LITTERATURARBETET I EUROPA

Tri-Division Publishing Council, 1971—Sweden. Publishing leaders of three
European divisions met to lay plans for strengthening and expanding the
publishing mission of the church throughout Europe.

After this experience while Captain Havstein was at
home a literature evangelist called. The captain purchased
a copy of the volume entitled, *Bibelske Foredrag* (Lecture
on the Sabbath). As he read the book, he was impressed
to accept the seventh-day Sabbath, convinced that God is
serious regarding obedience.

Realizing that it would be impossible to keep the
Sabbath as a sea captain, he sold his whaling vessel and

[111] Seventh-day Adventist Encyclopedia, p. 1006.

bought a small farm. As yet he had not learned of a Seventh-
day Adventist Church, however, he and his wife were faithful
in keeping the Sabbath.

Sickness and disappointment were frequent visitors
at this little farm. Later the captain's wife told of the many
times she found her husband in earnest prayer in some quiet
place.

The captain's daughter and husband learned to love
the message in this strange book. The Holy Spirit was at
work. Soon a Seventh-day Adventist minister was guided
to this little farm, where seven persons were waiting for
baptism.

This was just the opening chapter in the unfolding
story of a sea captain's narrow escape from death, the visit of
a literature evangelist, the faithful working of the Holy Spirit,
and the encouragement of a minister. Ultimately nineteen
members and relatives of Captain Havstein's family rejoiced
in the Third Angel's Message found in the book *Bibelske
Foredrag*.[112]

You Must Sleep Eight More Nights

Iceland dominates the volcanic group of islands at the
edge of the Arctic Circle in the North Atlantic Ocean. The
surface of this group is dotted with more than one hundred
volcanic peaks. Iceland has the largest glacier in Europe,
Vatnajikull, covering 3,140 square miles. From this great
ice field flow deep racing rivers over some of earth's most
spectacular falls.[113]

On one of Iceland's small island groups, known as
the Westman Islands, lived a young girl and her small brother
with their parents, who had left their Norwegian homeland

[112] Story told by Pastor Frithjof Aasheim, Publishing Director, East Norway Conference.
[113] The World Encyclopedia, Vol 10, pp. 16 & 17, 1968.

in 1924 to become missionaries to Iceland. There they spent thirty-three years.

There were no stores on their small island. Twice each year the parents traveled to the main island of Iceland to buy groceries and supplies. When the author visited Iceland he met the father, Pastor O.J. Olsen, [known as Iceland Olsen]*. He told the following story of faith:

> After telling the children goodbye, my wife and I left for the main island. The children would be left alone for many days. Bravely they watched as we walked toward the open sea where we would use a small boat to reach the mainland. It was very cold so they closed the door and watched through a window.

> The boy anxiously asked his sister, "How many days until Daddy returns?" His sister replied, "You must sleep eight more nights"

> The young lad went to his bedroom where he drew eight bold marks on his bedroom wall. Each morning when he awakened he would draw a line across one of the marks. The eighth morning he drew a line across the last mark, then went out on the front porch and began looking in the direction he had last seen us walking toward the sea. Late in the day, far in the distance, he saw two figures. Sure it was us, his parents, he was happy. He put on his heavy coat and boots, and hurried to meet us.

In concluding his story, Iceland Olsen said, "I painted my boy's bedroom wall several times after that, but I never painted over those eight marks of faith!"[114]

---

*Years later the author learned that Iceland Olsen was the uncle of his sister-in-law, Mary Ann Herwick Wickwire.
[114] Story told to author by Iceland Olsen.

Bishop Ends His Search

Iceland's Lutheran State Bishop had been searching
for Bible books for the children of Iceland. When he saw
the first copy of *The Bible Story* printed in Icelandic, he said,
"My search has ended. These will be the Bible books for
Iceland's youth."[115]

Curious Viking Moves to Wisconsin

Lois Sharpe, executive secretary and pastor's wife,
tells of her grandfather's experiences in the 1890s:[116]

Peter Hanson, a Lutheran minister in Norway
attended a ministerial convention in Oslo. He was warned
against the teachings of an Adventist preacher, John
Matteson. The discussion so aroused his curiosity that he
went to hear Matteson. The truths he heard convinced him to
accept the Seventh-day Adventist message.

Soon after becoming a Seventh-day Adventist Peter
Hanson immigrated to America with his family, and settled
in Chippewa Falls Valley, Wisconsin. Here he began many
years of service as a literature evangelist. He recorded some
of his early experiences as follows :

My first visit to Chippewa Falls Valley,
Wisconsin, was in the summer of 1895. I found
several Scandinavian settlements among the hills
on both sides of the river. I sold 745 *Prophecies
of Jesus*, and 211 *Thoughts on Daniel and the
Revelation*. Three years later I again visited these
settlements. Four persons were keeping the Sabbath.
Meetings and Bible studies were held in these
homes, and five more interested persons accepted the
Sabbath. I had twenty-four Bibles with me. They

[115] Told to author during 1969 Literature Evangelist Institute.
[116] In 2002, Lois Sharpe related this and other stories about her grandfather, Peter Hanson.

were soon sold, and I ordered more. Most of these people had the New Testament. Now they wanted the entire Bible. On this trip I also sold 427 copies of *The Great Controversy.*

Sole for Soul

On my way home, while waiting for the train in Eau Claire, I was walking back and forth on the train platform. The sole of one of my shoes caught against a projecting nail and tore loose. I went to a shoe store to have it fixed. The shoemaker suggested I would be money ahead if I bought a new pair of shoes. Since I had a copy of *The Great Controversy* in my satchel, I showed him the book. He seemed just as anxious to get *The Great Controversy*, as I was to get a new pair of shoes. We made an even exchange. The shoe repair man read *The Great Controversy*, accepted the Seventh-day Adventist message and became a faithful member of the church.

Grandpa's "Heresy Book"

Lois Sharpe further relates:[117] In 1895 Grandpa Peter Hanson was staying at the home of a well-known Scandinavian family while canvassing in that area. Shortly after he made a large delivery of *The Great Controversy,* one of his customers discovered reference in the book to keeping the seventh day as Sabbath. This man began an organized campaign, going from home to home to inform others about the "Sabbath heresy". They arranged a set time to confront Grandpa at his rooming house.

Learning from his host about what time Grandpa could be expected, they all arrived with their books and

[117]Story by Lois Sharpe

began stacking them on the dining room table. What a shock awaited Grandpa! A score of buggies lined the road, and inside was a stack of books and a row of angry faces.

"This book is full of heresy," the spokesman began, "and we all want our money back!"

"It is?" Grandpa calmly replied. "Now, I wasn't aware of that. I certainly wouldn't want to be selling a book with heresy in it. Show me where it is."

The spokesman found the page and read, "The Bible points to the seventh day, not to the first, as the Lord's day."

Grandpa looked intently at the passage, then observed. "There are Bible references at the bottom of the page. Suppose we look them up and see how they read. Does anyone have a Bible?"

A Bible was brought, and all gathered around to see what the texts said. There was mutual agreement that the passage in question agreed with the Scriptures.

"But just listen to this," continued the complainer. "'How utterly revolting is the belief that as soon as the breath leaves the body, the soul of the impenitent is consigned to the flames of hell!' Now, Elder Hanson, surely you will not deny the Bible teaching of hell?"

Grandpa studied the passage thoughtfully and again suggested they look up the texts given at the bottom of the page. By this time, nearly everyone was looking over another's shoulder to read the texts. One by one these persons began to leave, taking their books with them. When books and buggies had all disappeared, Grandpa's host turned to him and asked, "Did you say that I might have a copy of that book?"

Which One Was My Guardian Angel?

Lois Sharpe continues:[118] "What would you think if I bought an automobile?" asked my seventy-year old grandfather, speaking to his friend, L. H. Christian, who smiled as he replied, "If you get a car, be sure to get life insurance, too." Until this time Grandfather had driven a horse and buggy or spring wagon. At state campmeetings in the 1890's Grandfather's spring wagon, loaded with books, was the Adventist Book Center.

Grandfather bought a car and learned to drive it. One autumn day in 1925 he was returning for an evening Bible study after a day of visiting. Time was running short so he chose a logging road that would save him several miles. Above the rumble of the wheels on the washboard road, his strong voice carried out over the prairies a song that was in his heart:

He leadeth me! O blessed thought!
O words with heavenly comfort fraught!
What'ere I do, where'ere I be
Still 'tis God's hand that leadeth me!

Seeking Divine Guidance

The rumble of the wheels stopped, the engine began to stall, and the car was slowing down. The wheels were slipping in mud caused by a recent rain. Farther ahead it was worse, but there was no way to turn around. His little car came to a complete stop in mud up to the running board, then tipped to one side. Grandpa got out and tried to find a fence rail he could prop against the car. It was so thoroughly bogged down that it seemed nothing but a team of horses

[118]Story by Lois Sharpe

could pull it out. He scanned the prairies in every direction. No one was in sight. He couldn't remember having passed a house in miles. He decided to walk ahead to see if he could find help.

"Lord," he prayed, "This is an important Bible study tonight about the Sabbath question, and the people have invited their minister to join in. Please help me to be there on time, so I can uphold the truth."

When he returned to his car a bit later with a fence rail he had found along the way, he was surprised to see two men standing beside the car. One was dressed in overalls and the other in a business suit.

"May we help you?" they asked.

Grandpa replied, "It is useless to try to push it out, but if you can tell me where I can find a team . . . "

"You start the car, and we'll go behind and push," they said.

The little car was so deep in mud that Grandpa couldn't get to the crank, so setting the gas and spark levers, he sprawled out over the hood, reached down for the crank and gave it a quick pull. The engine responded. Now to try getting out while the men pushed. But then it would be useless. He had told them that! Back at the wheel, he was amazed at how quickly he gained solid ground. It felt as though the car had been lifted out because the wheels had not spun. It was like driving on pavement. He drove ahead a few feet to be sure, and then stopped to thank the men who had helped him.

He expected the men to be a few feet behind him, but no one was around. He could see for nearly a mile across the prairies. The only sound was the song of a meadowlark. He walked slowly back to the spot where his car had been. Yes, there was the clear imprint where it had rested, and there were his footprints, but no others. With a prayer of thankfulness he returned to his car. He no longer felt alone.

"Now just which one was my guardian angel?" he wondered.

"Hot Freight" Publicizes Meeting

Lois Sharpe narrates further:[119] In 1912 Grandfather teamed with Elder Post for a summer of tent meetings in northwestern Wisconsin. The large tent, benches, platform boards, and other equipment had been sent by freight to the town where the meetings were to be held. The local clergy, learning of the coming meetings, thoroughly warned their members against the Adventists.

The freight car with the equipment arrived ahead of the preachers and was left sealed on the sidetrack, awaiting payment of freight charges. In an attempt to stop the meetings, enemies learned of the freight car's contents and planned sabotage. Under cover of darkness they broke into the freight car, loaded the equipment onto a big hay wagon, then hurried off to hide it. From farmer to farmer they went, seeking permission to unload the equipment in a barn. No one wanted to be caught with "hot freight," so by morning it had to be returned and reloaded in the freight car.

The story was just too good to be kept secret and soon made the rounds of the town. When Grandfather and Elder Post arrived and set up the tent, the large attendance each evening astonished them. They soon learned the story of the "hot freight" and how it had publicized their meetings.

[119]Story by Lois Sharpe

Chapter 12 - Higher Education is Learning about People and Life

"It is not books, but men we must study." -- *Patrick Henry*

George Bush, Sr. as an officer on board ship said this about his duties: "As I did my duty I read other guy's mail, I learned about love, about heartbreak, about fear and courage, about the diversity of our great country." Then he said, "When I would see a man whose letter I had censored, I would look at him differently, look at him with more understanding. I gained an insight into the lives of my shipmates, and I felt richer."[120]

Contact with other minds is a polishing process for our own, sharpening our viewpoints and enlarging our general knowledge. A young student, who had come to the day of graduation with great joy, announced to the president of his college that he had finished his education. Replied the president, "I am just beginning mine."[121]

Divine foresight designed a scholarship plan for the church's future leaders. Beginning in the year 1907, the publishing ministry of the Seventh-day Adventist Church provided its youth with what may be termed a postgraduate course in soul-winning and public relations. From Union College students took doctrinal volumes proclaiming the message of the Three Angels to people living in towns, cities, and farming communities of the Midwest. With few exceptions, for the next ninety-four years, ministerial students, first in North America and later in other areas of the world, were invited, encouraged, and expected to acquire practical experience in meeting families by going from home to home. Studying the characters of men while presenting

---

[120] Tom Brokaw, The Greatest Generation, p. 273.
[121] J. D. Snider, Highways to Learning, p. 60.

the gospel provides an education that no one can take away.
Discovery is made that no person is greater than another,
except he does greater things.

In this information age formal education is
increasingly important. Men of learning, leaders of
thought, recognize the value of people meeting people as
a means of promoting human understanding. It is through
this experience that future pastors, teachers, and other
professionals develop a social and intellectual base for
service. "Academic training alone will never prepare a person
for the ministry," says Georgia-Cumberland Conference
Ministerial Director, Stan Patterson. The story entitled "The
Gift of a Simple Man," in Chapter 14 of this book, tells
how Stan and his brothers learned about the Seventh-day
Adventist Church.

Face-to-face gospel selling requires ability to listen
intelligently and to tailor words with meaning designed to
meet specific individuals and circumstances. "Every soul
is surrounded by an atmosphere of its own."[122] High above
surrounding tall buildings in New Jersey the writer saw this
motto: "We are a part of every person we have ever met."

Canvassing, Training for Ministry

Governments concerned for the welfare of their
nation, for readiness of young men and women who serve
their country, provide basic training before assigning
responsibility or a commission.

Young men and women divinely inspired to train for
the ministry do not expect their church to require less than the
best for their ministerial preparation. "Let young men show
that they have resting on them a burden from the Lord."[123]

---

[122] Christ's Object Lessons, p. 340. (1900), C.M., p. 67.
[123]Manuscript 75, 1900, C.M., p. 52.

A pastor, who as student literature evangelist, learned how to enter into the homes and hearts of strangers understands the importance and joy of making even brief pastoral visits, visits which water the pastor's own soul. Seeing members only from the pulpit deprives both pastor and member. Home visits often solve or prevent difficult problems.

A student canvasser has been provided one of life's important lessons when he has led a total stranger to invest a portion of his hard-earned money, not as a gift, but because he is convinced that the books and journals being demonstrated will provide answers to life's questions. Literature evangelism is the union of human effort with limitless divine power. Nothing can withstand it.

The path is not easy, "but work in the canvassing field will do more than almost anything else to prepare young men for the ministry, after they have had opportunity to become Bible students."[124]

Don't bring me your successes, they make me weak. Bring me your problems, they make me strong.

•Anonymous

A Lesson From an Old Shepherd

A familiar folk story tells of an old shepherd suddenly made ruler of his people. That he not forget his roots and his people, he annually removed his royal robe, put on his shepherd's mantle and sandals, and with shepherd's staff in hand left the comforts of royal office to spend time with his people where they lived, labored, struggled and died.

Similarly publishing directors are encouraged to annually spend one or two weeks in direct gospel selling to

[124]Ellen G. White letter 132, to Brother Irwin, August 17, 1902.

keep in tune with times and needs. If each church leader would take time and follow the old shepherd's formula the church would experience a reformation. Membership would increase as would tithes and offerings.

Denominational Officers' Commission

Sizes and styles to fit almost everyone.

Seventh-day Adventist laymen who ask, "What happened to North American Division's successful literature evangelism program?" agree that "the presidents of our conferences and others in responsible positions have a duty to do . . . that the different branches of our work may receive equal attention. Canvassers are to be educated and trained to do the work required in selling the books upon present truth which the people need."[125] Laymen are the church. As such they expect encouragement and recognition of God's call to become a literature evangelist.

Books such as *The Great Controversy, Desire of Ages* and *Patriarchs and Prophets"* are especially adapted to give enlightenment and encouragement to those who have newly come to the faith. As future pastors acquaint themselves with the contents of these volumes, they begin to comprehend the divine effect their message has upon human hearts and minds.

---

[125] Testimonies, Vol. 6, p. 329 (1900).

Confidence – Self Assurance

The late educator Orison Swett Marden in a baccalaureate address once said regarding student experience in book canvassing,

I have seen a young college student so completely changed by his experience in book canvassing during the vacation following his freshman year that you would scarcely have recognized him.   Confidence and self-assurance had taken the place of timidity and self-consciousness. He had developed initiative. His work forced him to become a good conversationalist – to state his opinions clearly and convincingly. Also his experience had taught him a great deal about human nature, for he was forced to study people, to learn to read them, that he might be able to approach different types of men and women in different ways, each according to his peculiar temperament. If a certain amount of canvassing were obligatory in all our colleges and higher institutions of learning, I believe it would be a good thing, because it would develop resourcefulness and inventiveness; it would show students a side of their nature which college courses cannot touch. It is well known that many students who pay their way in college by vacation canvassing develop a remarkable practical power, which students whose expenses are paid by their parents do not develop.

Definite Four Year Advantage
"Four Years Ahead"

In an issue of the New York SUN we found this statement:

That freshman who takes up some form

of vacation canvassing and gets out and meets the people is four years ahead of his fellows who do not. The success of our dealings with one another . . . depends upon the quality of our salesmanship, upon how we impress those to whom we talk. Vacation salesmanship brings out the best there is in a boy or girl and affords an excellent opportunity to put to test and to practical uses the training of the nine months of school.

Former U. S. Senator J. B. Foraker was himself a vacation book salesman while in college. In addressing students at Delaware, Ohio he said, "Young man, you should not be entitled to your diploma until you have at least canvassed one summer. Your education is not complete without the experience."

"If the iron be blunt, and he do not whet the edge, then must he put to more strength: but wisdom is profitable. .
."[126]

Testimony of a Successful Adventist Doctor:

"Are you interested in our regular or de luxe edition?"

A super-salesman? Not I! But I grew up faster, learned more about public relations, earned more money, and developed more faith in God's leading and providences as a student literature evangelist than in anything else I could ever have done! I canvassed four summers, and earned four scholarships. -- D. S. Small, M. D.

The servant of the Lord said many years ago, "The

---

[126]Ecclesiastes 10:10

very best education young men can obtain is by entering the canvassing field and working from house to house."[127]

From the writer's contact with young people it has been discovered that any student who feels divinely called to serve the Lord will accept the opportunity to not only be schooled in theory but also be field-trained.

Great care is required in selecting and training young men and women to minister to church members before being given denominational recognition with a voice of authority.

Faced with a given set of problems one man may tackle them with intelligence, grace and courage; another may react with resentment; a third may run away altogether. In any life, facts tend to remain unyielding. But attitudes are a matter of choice – and that choice is up to you. "When facts won't budge, you have to bend your attitudes to fit them."[128]

One Brave Salesman

From the author's contact with students during gospel sales training institutes at Newbold College he became acquainted with two students who decided to go to Iceland, the land of fire and ice, for a summer of evangelistic sales effort.

Upon arrival by ship in Iceland they learned that the price of fish, Iceland's principle source of income, was down. One student, when he heard of the drop in Iceland's economy, decided to remain on the ship and return to England.

The other student said, "God's work is not dependent on the price of fish." He spent the summer selling gospel literature and returned to Newbold with **two** scholarships.

[127] Manuscript 75, 1900, C.M., p. 32.
[128] Arthur Gordon, Touch of Wonder, p. 197.

Big Books Equals Good Day

As people search for an escape from life's near oppressive marketing rage, they want calm and a chance to be heard. Seated inside a stranger's home, literature evangelists have opportunity to listen to crying hearts. By sincere listening they gain deep insight into humanity. People who say they are too busy are often lonesome and want to express life's burdens. They thank the literature evangelist for knocking at their door and for listening.

It is in big book selling that the maximum exchange of thought is experienced.

"Any day that I get to canvass Big Books is a good day!" states upbeat Ruth Heinemann. I like her optimism. Ruth is a student at SOULS [Southern Outreach Leadership School]. She canvassed with Big Books during the summer. ['Big Books' is a term used by students as opposed to MagaBooks.] Ruth has also spent previous summers selling MagaBooks. This past summer, selling Big Books, she averaged over $1,000 per week in processed sales. It was all door-to-door and referrals.[129]

Greater Value Than Years in Classroom

Pastor John Arthur, former British Union Conference president, executive director of ADRA-Trans Europe, and presently publishing director of the Trans European Division, states: "I have had the privilege of working for the church for thirty-nine years with a variety of portfolios."

His various work assignments have caused him to meet heads of state, prime ministers, ambassadors, and aid agency presidents. He counts a visit to Buckingham Palace

[129] Reported by Bill Beckworth, Publishing Director, Southern Union Conference, in Southern Union Literature Evangelist Newsletter, October 24, 2001.

where he talked briefly with Her Majesty Queen Elizabeth II, the Duke of Edinburgh and the Princess Royal, a most memorable occasion

Prior to entering college, and during five summer vacations, Pastor Arthur engaged in literature evangelism. In speaking of his canvassing work he says, "This experience of meeting people from all walks of life, together with the development of persuasion skills, financial and time management, and general self-discipline were of greater value to me personally than the years spent in the classroom."[130]

What I Learned in One Summer
The Scholarship Plan is Worldwide

Dr. Humberto M. Rasi, director of the world's largest protestant educational system, the Seventh-day Adventist school system, in sharing with Adventist youth secrets for success, tells his experience in gospel selling:

In the early part of my senior year at an Adventist boarding academy in Argentina, I decided to go on to college and become a teacher. I knew that my parents, who had been providing financial support for my studies, would not be able to increase their assistance. Thus, the idea of spending the summer selling Adventist publications and earning my college scholarship seemed an attractive option.

Dr. Humberto M Rasi.

---

[130] Letter dated 12 July 1999 from W. John Arthur, Publishing Director, Trans European Division.

He enrolled in the student literature evangelist club, where through monthly instructional sessions he learned the techniques of approaching people and interesting them in acquiring Seventh-day Adventist books and journals. He and his friends practiced their canvasses on each other until they became thoroughly familiar with the book prospectus they would use. They staged sales presentations, learning how to respond to clients' objections. Excitement increased!

Before the school year was over those who were to go canvassing were assigned partners and a sales territory . Humberto Rasi's partner, Pablo, was a mature college senior who was going out for the sixth time and who each year had earned his scholarship. Pablo kept a careful countdown of the days until the end of the summer canvassing session and to his wedding day.

Humberto kept a journal of his experiences, the emotional ups-and-downs, surprises, loneliness, and successes. He says, "That summer, at 18, I learned seven values and habits that would help me through the rest of my life:
Friendship with God,
People skills,
Organization,
Adaptability,
Resource management,
Perseverance, and
Self-confidence."

He further stated, "That summer, as a student literature evangelist, I earned not only my freshman college scholarship but also a half-scholarship for my younger brother. Above all, I learned that when the human will submits to and joins with God's will, they become invincible."[131]

[131] By Humberto M. Rasi, Director, Dept. of Education, General Conference of Seventh-day Adventists, published October-December 1997, in GC Publishing Department Literature Evangelist.

I Shall Never Forget

In 1948 when the writer accepted the invitation of the church to serve as Publishing Director of the Dutch East Indies, now Indonesia, he took a very special memory with him. It was the memory of dozens of student literature evangelists going from door-to-door and selling on busy streets, presenting the message of salvation to strangers. One summer in Texas publishing department leaders recruited and trained one hundred wonderful students. I remembered how they met challenges and won. They sold books and magazines by the thousands. Some of those very students are today's respected Seventh-day Adventist editors, administrators and TV evangelists. Others entered the world of business, and some dealt with the nation's vast grain market. All testify that student canvassing experiences molded and enriched their lives. The church can be proud of its brave young people who invest mental and physical capital in preparation for service to the church.

Transfusion

In earlier days student literature evangelists walked, rode bicycles, rode horseback or traveled in horse drawn buggies or covered wagons. As used cars became available, students chose this method of transportation. Sometimes two students traveled together in the same car.

The author recalls two students who used an old model car while canvassing. As they traveled about on their gospel mission, they left behind a dark vapor trail. People might imagine they were trying to rid their territory of mosquitoes. Not so. They were driving an oil-burning machine. Being resourceful young men, they carried a supply of used oil in quart jars in the trunk of their car.

Literature evangelists often accepted farm produce, canned goods, chickens, geese, eggs, and other items in exchange for their books and journals. One day these young men received quart jars of sorghum molasses as payment for the books they left with a family. They put the jars of molasses safely in the trunk of their car. At dusk with a number of calls yet to make, the car needed another transfusion of oil. One of the young men applied a quart of what he assumed was used oil. Their thirsty engine was given its transfusion. Imagine their consternation when back on the road they suddenly smelled the odor of scorched molasses! That sweet drink was the engine's last!

Why Some College Graduates Were Not Hired

Reports from 186 large companies in all parts of North America throw light on why some college graduates are turned down when they apply for their first jobs.

The companies were asked to list the factors that often lead to rejection of job hunters just out of college. Dr. Frank S. Endicott, Director of Placement at Northwestern University, tabulated replies. Major reasons for rejections were listed as follows:

1. Poor scholastic record in college. Low grades without reasonable explanation, a low level of accomplishment.
2. Inadequate personality – poor attitude, lack of self-confidence, timid, hesitant approach, introverted.
3. Lack of goals. Poorly motivated, does not know his interests.
4. Lack of enthusiasm and drive. Inability to sell himself.[132]

After a summer of canvassing the student may

[132] U. S. News and World Report, January 11, 1965.

well say, "I knew all save myself alone."

The Scholarship Plan, a Preparation for Success

The student who works as a literature evangelist during his vacation not only gains a liberal scholarship, but also learns to understand human nature. He learns to sell himself. Dwight L. Moody once said,

> Now young men, before you are thoroughly equipped for your life work, I would advise you to spend two or three months in selling and introducing some high-class publication. There is nothing that will give you an insight into human nature and a store of practical knowledge such as this occupation can afford.

Keeping the Scholarship Plan alive is a denominational safeguard against any student becoming a church leader [perhaps a dysfunctional leader] who lacks industry, promptness, cooperation, respect, teamwork, honesty, bravery, and loyalty. The Scholarship Plan is to the church what basic military training is to a nation's army. It provides lessons for the wise use of authority. It is not a numbers process but a valuable evaluation process.

Timeless Counsel

Ellen G. White has provided enduring guidance for students:

> Let those who have been in school go out into the field and put to a practical use the knowledge they have gained. If canvassers will do this, using the ability which God has given them, seeking counsel from Him, and combining the work of selling

books with personal labor for the people, their talents will increase by exercise, and they will learn many practical lessons which they could not possibly learn in school. The education obtained in this practical way may properly be termed higher education.[133]

"I have had special light in regard to canvassing work, and the impression and burden does not leave me. This work is a means of education."[134]

An Invaluable Experience
Observing the Holy Spirit in Action

In each gospel sales transaction the Holy Spirit is present to awaken a divine homing instinct. It is the Holy Spirit that gives words to speak to people of different religions and temperaments.

Ellen G. White again counsels:
All who desire an opportunity for true ministry, and who will give themselves unreservedly to God, will find in the canvassing work opportunities to speak upon many things pertaining to the future, immortal life. The experience thus gained will be of the greatest value to those who are fitting themselves for the ministry. It is the accompaniment of the Holy Spirit of God that prepares workers, both men and women, to become pastors to the flock of God.[135]

Nothing Great is Easily Won

Success is not the result of an accident. Selling is a specialized field of activity. No person is a natural born salesperson. Preparation and experience are necessary. The beginning salesman quickly learns that good looks,

[133] Testimonies, Vol. 6, pp. 330, 331 (1900), C.M., pp. 32, 33.
[134] Manuscript 26, 1901, C.M., pp. 31, 32.
[135]Testimonies, Vol. 6, p. 322. (1900), C.M., p. 33.

prominent name, fast talking, or good connections are no substitute for preparation.

Classroom salesmanship provides the student with some understanding of what to expect in meeting potential customers so that later he will experience fewer surprise situations.

As the church enters earth's final moments church members expect their sons and daughters, properly trained, to lead the people of God across the finish line. In this late moment of earth's history, responsibility should not be misunderstood, delayed or ignored.

To Risk, To Dare

In his book *No Higher Calling,* the late Joseph N. Hunt, one of the churches' most professional and successful publishing department directors, left a message for Seventh-day Adventist youth. He tells how years ago God asked him to give up his own plans and risk a summer in literature evangelism. He had no father to guarantee his school expenses, and it seemed safer to take a definite wage-per-hour job on an Iowa farm or at the academy broom factory, however he decided to answer the Lord's call. His teachers thought he would return home in a few weeks' time. A friend refused to be his partner, explaining, "I want to make sure I get back to school next fall." Joe concluded his story by saying, "After five summers of wonderful blessings as a student literature evangelist and finishing college debt-free, I learned that God never calls

Joseph N. Hunt

162 GOSPEL IN SHOES

to failure. Whatever we risk for His cause He repays us a hundredfold."[136]

Joe Hunt, one of the associates in the General Conference Publishing Department, was involved in a serious accident while on the mission of the church. While doctors struggled to save his life, telephone calls came to the hospital's surgery theatre from around the world inquiring, "Can you save him? We are praying for him." Doctors asked, "Who is this man? He must be very important."

Wherever Elder Joe Hunt went in the world he caused gospel light to shine. Though he did not survive, his influence lives on through the thousands touched by his lifelong publishing ministry, which began as a student literature evangelist.

An Attorney's Story

The oldest of seven brothers, Attorney Thomas R. Knoll was seventeen years of age when a literature evangelist visited the family home in the early 1940s and enrolled his mother in a Voice of Prophecy Bible correspondence course. After completing the Bible course, the family attended an evangelistic series of meetings and were baptized. Today all of their families are members of the Seventh-day Adventist Church.

After his baptism Thomas became a student literature evangelist and continued canvassing for seven summers. The Lord blessed with success from the beginning. During one of those summers at a student colporteur rally Thomas met Merry, who later became his wife. He says, "I owe everything to the Lord through the publishing ministry, my Christian experience, my family, and a Christian education."

[136] Joseph N. Hunt, No Higher Calling, p. 87.

Thomas R. Knoll, Sr.
Attorney at Law

Thomas completed college and seminary training, then served as a pastor, a public evangelist, and for five years as publishing director in Ontario, Canada. During those five years his office supervised 150 student literature evangelists each summer. Many of these students are now leaders in the church as ministers, doctors, lawyers, teachers and other professions. Thomas says, "It is a pleasure to meet and reminisce about how the Lord blessed those students in those days now gone by. Only eternity will reveal the full impact of their endeavors."

Imagine the results of five years of publishing work in Ontario, Canada. In addition to regular full-time literature evangelists, there were 150 students each summer for five years. Think of the thousands of families visited by 750 students as they sold books, prayed in the homes and enrolled hundreds in Bible courses.

After returning to the United States, Thomas took the law course and became an attorney. Speaking of the value of the student scholarship plan and its impact on his life, Attorney Knoll says:

As a practicing attorney, each time I enter a court room I am reminded that the Lord has prepared me for this profession through my canvassing experience. When I make my case to the judge, I am reminded of giving a Bible study, presenting a sermon, or giving a canvass. When I present my closing argument, I am always reminded of my canvassing experience and calling for the order. I thank the Lord for my experience as a student literature evangelist.[137]

It is reasonable to believe that field-tested Attorney Thomas R. Knoll, a master salesman, seldom loses a legal case. He learned how to study the characters and thoughts of men, and thus became equipped to represent clients in courts of justice.

"The canvassing work is more important than many have regarded it."[138]

The Big Book

Elder Roy Adams, currently one of the Seventh-day Adventist church's able writers, tells how the message of the Three Angels was brought to his attention. "I will never forget the 'big book' that some Adventist colporteur left in the home of my Roman Catholic cousins. . . Only eternity will reveal how many lives have been changed by millions of these quiet witnesses left in hands and homes across the years."[139]

On The South Dakota Prairie

Beverly Holweger, Women's Ministries Director for the Georgia-Cumberland Conference, tells of her father's days as a colporteur. "At that time, late 1930's and 40's, colporteuring was the training field for young men who felt called into ministry. It was there they learned to trust God for daily bread, literally. Those were very hard times. Our family had no car. My dad, E. T. Gackenheimer, set out on foot, through all kinds of weather, on the South Dakota prairie, selling truth filled literature."[140]

---

[137]E-mail, 19 Feb. 2002 from Attorney Thomas R. Knoll.
[138] Testimonies, Vol. 5, p. 406 (1885) C.M., p. 26.
[139] Adventist Review, October 10, 1996, p. 5.
[140] Letter from Beverly Holweger to the author, 2003.

Elder Gackenheimer's life was committed to the church. The challenges he met in his work as a literature evangelist prepared him for fruitful years of gospel service at home and in lands afar.

"Dakota Returns to Historic Beginnings"

"Dakota News" in the April 2003 Mid-America Outlook gives the following report: "The Adventist message was originally spread throughout the conference due largely to the literature work. Thanks to a donor who believes in the literature work, once again the Dakota Adventist Academy has started a Magabook program."[141] The story reveals that two pastors, former literature evangelists, assisted in training the young people in the science of personal contact with the public.

Spirit of Dedication Moves Church

"In the fall of 2001, the Hurley [South Dakota] church made a decided effort to reach out to others. With the goal of rededication as their focus of ministry and united efforts of Bible study and literature evangelism, the members saw the results of their efforts in a very short time. . . Church growth seemed to snowball."

The above "Dakota News" article pictures six individuals who joined the Hurley church through baptism. The caption, "The year 2002 was full of growth and excitement. . ."[142]

Busy in the Kingdom!

In recording the soul-winning stories in this book the

[141] Mid America Outlook, Dakota News, April 2003.
[142] Ibid.

writer is convinced that in the new earth literature evangelists
will be busy meeting persons in whose homes they visited,
prayed and sold gospel literature. No one will regret the price
paid for soul-saving books/journals.

1918 Dedication

Eighty-six years ago C. H. Spurgeon spoke of
scholarships and colporteurs thus:

To our friends, the workers;
To the girls and boys who have earned their
scholarships;
To the forty-hour-per-week colporteurs;
To the thrifty who earn their money before they spend
it –
This little book, with its quaint sayings and proverbs,
is dedicated.[143]

[143] C. H. Spurgeon, John Ploughman's Talks, p.v., Review and Herald Publishing
Association.

Chapter 13 – Just a Colporteur

A Man Named Waller

There is little, if any, real estate on earth where the footprints of literature evangelists are not found. In areas that are believed to have no known Adventist presence Seventh-day Adventist literature evangelists have already entered.

Madam, for a moment you startled me! I thought you was Hedy Lamarr!

This story began in Dixon, Mississippi about 1900 with a man named Waller,[144] a colporteur. We do not know his first name, only his initials, J. L. What is important is that he was about his Master's business selling the book, *Bible Footlights*. Among the many families to whom Waller sold copies of his book was W. E. Cooper, whose sister was Sarah Ann McKee. Sarah Ann and her husband read the book.

In 1918 Sarah Ann McKee and her husband, Finis, at the invitation of Mr. Cooper, were baptized and joined the Seventh-day Adventist Church. This was the beginning of a lifelong loyalty to the Three Angels' Message discovered in the book *Bible Footlights*.

With commitment to the teachings of the church came conviction regarding the importance of Christian education. A storage area above the family operated general store became a church school for their children and others. This interest in Christian education has been evident through succeeding generations of the McKee family.

In the spring of 1921 a colporteur boarded with Finis

[144]Read about Literature Evangelist Waller in "So Many Lion's Roaring", by C. A. Oliphant, p. 47.

and Sarah Ann McKee. Many evenings he told exciting stories about his canvassing work. The children were enthralled with his tales, so much that one son, O. D. (as he was affectionately known) begged to be allowed to "go out and canvass." He exhausted his parents with his pleading, until finally his father, Finis, said, "Let him go. He will be back in two weeks." His mother, who had strongly resisted his desires, relented and gave him thirty dollars as he started off to his mission.

Two months later O. D. returned home. He had fulfilled his commitment to work two full months. He was not a quitter. He canvassed succeeding summers selling enough to earn scholarships to Southern Junior College (now Southern Adventist University) not only for himself but also for his brother, A. D.

O. D. McKee, Founder and Benefactor of McKee Foods.

A double measure of sales experience is revealed in the McKee Baking Company success story. Life teaches that nothing great is easily won. O. D. learned important lessons in the human school of experience, which developed a solid base for his future. His spirit to fulfill a commitment was lived out in his personal and business life.

Sometime ago the writer spoke with Ellsworth McKee, son of O. D. McKee about my desire to include the McKee Baking Company success story in this book. I said, "With such phenomenal success there has to be some stable business minds under girding it." Ellsworth, at that time president of McKee Baking Company, quickly responded, "And the blessings of heaven." When human effort trusts in the divine, success is certain.

Building a bakery empire, which began as a small operation, was not without ups and downs. Character lessons O. D. had learned as a student colporteur stood him in good stead. In July 1996 a Chattanooga, Tennessee newspaper, _News Leader,_ reported on the vastness of the McKee Foods Corporation and its several production plants. With 4,500 employees and a sales volume in the hundreds of millions of dollars, it has become a rapidly expanding business.

As you travel America's interstate highways, expect to see one or more of the hundreds of McKee Baking Company "eighteen wheelers," each bearing large, clear symbols, LITTLE DEBBIE. These trucks will be loaded with approximately thirty tons of bakery goods, weighed out by computer. Long before sunset on Friday factories are closed, the vast parking lots at factories located in three states are filled with eighteen wheelers, the diesel engines silent and the drivers at rest. There is quietness. It is Sabbath!

The McKee family does not forget its "publishing" roots.

Finis Laverne McKee, fifth of seven children, was born on his father's birthday, thus inherited his father's name. Finis, a lifelong colporteur, brother of O. D. A. D., John, and A. C. went to his rest after over thirty years of sowing gospel seed. He, too, was committed to the trust, _"he that goeth forth and weepeth, bearing precious seed, shall doubtless come again rejoicing, bearing his sheaves with him."_[145]

Each of the McKee brothers gave a portion of his life to the literature ministry, and each now rest in the Collegedale Memorial Park, within the shadow of the Plant 2 of the McKee Foods Corporation. Somehow I imagine that among the first persons they will want to meet and thank in heaven will be literature evangelist Waller, dismissed by some individuals as "**just a colporteur.**" Waller was, in fact

[145]Psalms 126:6.

a very influential man.   In the area of Dixon, Mississippi, fifteen families he had visited, prayed with, and sold books to, became Seventh-day Adventists. His literature evangelistic efforts influenced dozens of other families in three or more states.

Richard McKee, son of Finis Laverne McKee, a career literature evangelist and publishing director, has served the church on a worldwide basis. While serving overseas, he was impressed with the benefits that would come from having literature ministry seminaries around the world. Today these schools, twenty in number, operate in Africa, Russia, North America, the Orient and other areas. This plan has been especially encouraged and strengthened by the generosity of the McKee family and by other men and women of means and world vision.

Literature evangelist Waller neither realized, nor could he imagine the far-reaching influence of just one visit and the message of just one book, *Bible Footlights*. By faith he believed that "the canvassing work properly conducted is missionary work of the highest order . . ."[146]

Literature evangelist Waller was somewhat like the Galilean disciples who were called "**just fisherman.** Through the vision and supportive influence of the vast McKee Baking Company his footprints are evident in the publishing, education and other ministries of the worldwide Seventh-day Adventist Church.[147]

World Vision

Land developer William (Bill) Hulsey, Mayor of Collegedale, Tennessee, shared with the author stories and pictures of literature evangelism seminary buildings in Africa. He told of personal visits to inspect and select sites

[146] Testimonies, Vol. 6, p. 313, (1900), C.M., pp. 6, 7.
[147] Read the McKee story in "Sweet Success" by C. A. Oliphant.

for Africa's publishing ministry training centers. Mr. Hulsey is an industrialist whose business acumen, advice, and support is evident in various major church ministries.

Marvin McColpin, whose wife Rose had been a life-long literature evangelist, was also a land developer with special interest in Literature Evangelist Training Centers, making trips abroad to determine need and ensure wise investments. After his wife's death he remarried. Faye, his new companion, shares his publishing interests, especially the need for a publishing house in Russia. One day the writer met Mr. McColpin on his way to the bank. He said, "I want to personally make this additional large gift for the Russian Publishing House before I die." Since his death his wife, Faye, continues their interest in publishing. She has traveled to Russia to observe results of their investment. On one of her recent visits she purchased a van for use in transporting literature evangelists to and from their territories.

Linked with the Great Teacher

While college graduates enter the literature ministry, others with limited classroom training may appear destitute of the knowledge obtained in school yet be purpose-driven, consecrated to God, and allow God to work through them. Like the disciples when called from their nets to follow Christ, they learn precious lessons from the Saviour. They link themselves with the Great Teacher, and the knowledge they gain from the Scriptures qualifies them to speak to others of Christ.

"The knowledge of the most learned man, if he has not learned in Christ's school, is foolishness so far as leading souls to Christ is concerned."[148] God works with those who respond to the invitation, "Whom shall I send, and who will go for Us?[149]

[148] Testimonies, Vol. 6, p. 318, (1900).
[149] Isaiah 6:8.

A Man Named Bradford

Theodore T. Jones, Associate Secretary of the General Conference of Seventh-day Adventists, tells the following story in the pages of the Adventist Review:

In 1951, during the Christmas holiday season, I visited my grandparents' home in Hutchinson, Kansas. I happened to be up in the attic of the old house, and discovered some large books covered with dust.

As I dusted the volumes I discovered the books were entitled *The Great Controversy Between Christ and Satan*, *The Desire of Ages*, *The Sanctified Life*, and *Patriarchs and Prophets* – all written by Ellen G. White. These were old books, large and heavy. When I took them downstairs and placed them on the dining room table, my maternal grandmother told me this story:

Charles E. (Brad) Bradford,
Administrator and Writer.
"The Preachers' Preacher."

A man named Bradford sold books from saddlebags on his horse. He sold a set of books to my grandfather's mother. She read and studied the books while living in Norborne, Missouri, and became a Seventh-day Adventist. She and her husband had six children, five girls and one boy. All five girls became Seventh-day Adventists, but the one son did not join the church.

That son, my grandfather, continued to be exposed to the seeds of truth. Five years after he died my mother and grandmother made their decisions to join the Adventist

Church after completing a Voice of Prophecy Bible study course. By that time I, too, had been exposed to the gospel through the influence of my extended family, who were Seventh-day Adventists. That gospel seed sprouted into my own call to pastoral ministry and later to the ministry of the printed page.

My great-grandmother was initially attracted to this church by the clear and systematic way that Seventh-day Adventists understand the Bible, especially the Bible prophecies about last-day events. The man who sold her those books was an ancestor of Charles Bradford, retired president of the Seventh-day Adventist Church in North America.

Our church has its roots in Bible prophecy, and I am convinced that God is still leading a people out of this dark world into the marvelous light of His truth.[150]

The Visit of a Tall Young Man

Born prior to the Great Depression, Merle Gates worked as a boy from sunup to sundown on his father's Pennsylvania farm. When hired out to work for neighbor, his wages were fifty cents for a long hard day. Money was scarce. When he asked his father for a dollar to take a girl out on a date, the response was, "What do you need a dollar for?"

When Merle was twenty-two he decided that the depression obligated him to seek non-farm employment. He persuaded the mail carrier to write a letter recommending him to the U S Army. He was accepted into peacetime military service with a reliable income. When his military service was completed he returned home and married his sweetheart.

[150] Adventist Review, September 17, 2001, p. 16.

In the Providence of God some interesting things
began to happen. A tall young man selling Christian
literature stopped at the Gates Pennsylvania farmhouse and
knocked at the kitchen screen door. When he left the home,
he left behind copies of *Bible Readings for the Home* and *The
Great Controversy*.

Merle's son, Richard Gates, a missionary, publishing
house manager, teacher, nurse, and mission pilot, takes up
the story:

> My grandmother and her daughter Evelyn
> found truth in those books. Soon they were baptized
> and began to spread the good news! Neither of my
> parents were high school graduates, but my mother
> was full of questions. My young Aunt Evelyn
> answered their questions with God's Word. Both Dad
> and Mother were baptized when I was two years old.

> Of the five brothers only my Dad (Merle) cast
> his lot with the Seventh-day Adventist Church, but
> what a difference it made to him and to subsequent
> generations.

The story takes up again in the early 60's after
Richard was married:

> Meraldine and I with two little toddlers,
> boarded a plane for Bolivia, encouraged by the
> commitment of both sets of parents to be brave and
> face the unknown.

> I wrote lots of letters home and in one asked
> Dad and Mom about an urgent need to buy a property
> in a little jungle town in Eastern Bolivia where the
> Adventist message was unknown. We had been
> invited to start work in this little town of ox carts and
> dirt streets.

Dad approached the executor of his Mother's estate, and inquired about an advance withdrawal of his inheritance. He received $8.000.00. That was what he had worked so hard for so long. Now it was to be given to God.

He was happy to do it, for he loved others as he loved himself. His funds were sufficient for a down payment on a property where a church, a clinic and living quarters were built. Over one hundred people were baptized during the years we spent in that place.

Sacrifice is heaven's secret joy. Dad gladly gave his inheritance of $8,000.00, but what an inheritance he will have awaiting him at the resurrection! [151]

Only a Short Step – Counsel of a General Conference President

C. H. Watson, former General Conference President, believed that,

Every leader who fails to recognize the fruitfulness of literature is making a great mistake. It is **only a short step** from the time the literature work is allowed to drop in a field, that the drop will be felt in the soul winning in that field. . . Let your literature work go on, regardless of conditions, and your soul winning will go on. . .

Financially the literature work is self-supporting. Effectively, it is abundantly fruitful. Evangelistically, it is wonderfully direct and effectual, and it is to be observed that the men and women who

---

[151] Contributed by Richard Gates, son of Merle Gates.

have been won to the movement by our literature
are usually firm and satisfactory Seventh-day
Adventists.[152]

In The Wake of Literature Ministry

This message from L. C. Naden, former president of
the South Pacific Division:
> The literature ministry has been a must from
> the beginning of our work. The success of our soul
> winning program in Australia . . . must be attributed
> largely to the prominent part literature evangelism has
> played in these lands down under the Southern Cross.
> Successful evangelistic campaigns always followed
> in the wake of literature ministry . . . Some of our
> most successful workers have told with pride how
> forebears accepted the message through reading some
> of these books."[153]

The Angel Said Australia

In a meeting being held in the Battle Creek, Michigan
church in 1875, Mrs. E. G. White related details of a vision
she had received in January of that year. She said there were
unthought-of fields where the Word was to be preached, and
where papers were to be printed. When asked if she could
name the countries, she said, "I remember the angel said
Australia."[154]

In May of 1888 self-supporting literature evangelist
William Arnold returned to England from Australia where
he had sold 2,168 copies of *Thoughts on Daniel and the
Revelation* and other books. He had made contact with
lawyers, doctors, leading ministers, and members of
parliament as well as businessmen.

[152]E. R. Palmer, The Printing Press and the Gospel, p. 145.
[153]Ibid., pp. 143, 144
[154]S. Ross Goldstone, The Angel Said Australia, p. 8.

The church in South Australia was growing. When Joseph Steed and his wife, who operated a hardware store and a house decorating business in Adelaide, made their decision for the truth they met great hostility. Encouraged to go into literature evangelism to "help finish the work," Joseph went daily from home to home not only selling, but also winning souls. When he met someone who showed a real interest he maintained contact until that person rejoiced in truth received. For sixteen years he continued this gospel work in South Australia, leaving lights burning in towns and villages.

Papa, Come Home

Many times 'Papa' as he was affectionately called by his brave little wife, would be away for months at a time. This situation reached its peak on one occasion when she heard the neighbor's children asking her children where their father was. "He's dead," they replied. She then wrote her husband, "Papa, come home. Your family thinks you are dead." But he was alive to a great soul-saving work. Joseph Steed gave many years of dedicated ministry to the Adventist Church.[155]

Brave and often very lonely are wives and children of literature evangelists who are gone long days, often arriving home late at night. Some are away from family for weeks and even months. In the kingdom wives and children will surely share in the joy of souls won.

Working the Outback

Distances are vast in the "Outback" in Queensland, Australia. It is there that literature evangelist Arthur Bond worked for His Master for a number of years.[156]

[155] S. Ross Goldstone, The Angel Said Australia, pp. 66, 67.
[156] The author first heard this story in 1979 when he assisted in gospel sales meetings in Australia.

The Bonds usually arrive in their territory with
Mrs. Bond driving their car and pulling their house trailer
(caravan). Arthur Bond drives their truck, which had a 500-
gallon water supply, his office, and a book and magazine
supply. The first duty is to find a rancher who will allow the
Bonds to park their equipment, preferably under a large tree.
Immediately they establish a sanitary system.

Mrs. Bond, a teacher by profession, instructs their
four children by correspondence from kindergarten through
to university entrance. Class work runs on schedule. The
few ranch families in the sparsely settled area are soon
contacted, so each stay is brief at any location.

Literature evangelist Bond moves his family of six
approximately thirty times each year. In fourteen years the
family caravan has moved 420 times. They have opened and
closed thousands of gates.

A Mrs. Watts was receiving the *Signs of the Times*
magazine sold by Bond, and it was used to build fires. One
day as her son John started to build the fire, he was attracted
to one of the articles in the *Signs*. He didn't burn it but kept
the paper and read it. Through this *Signs* article he was led
to the truth regarding the seventh day Sabbath. He became
a Seventh-day Adventist and studied for the ministry at
Andrews University.

Only God could impress Arthur Bond to take his
family into the outback of Australia to proclaim the message
of God's love for man. There is but one answer; belief in a
divine call and mission.

The Queen's Outrider

In 1979, when the author visited Australia and New

Zealand, he met Henry Thompson, and heard him tell how he was once a defiant young seaman, who had jumped ship. Like Paul on the Damascus Road, he found Christ, and later became a literature evangelist. He told of his first transportation, a bicycle, and how he upgraded to a painted and repainted motorcycle.

For forty-two years he traveled from family to family in his literature ministry with more than 400 baptized as a result. He had become well-known in the area where he lived in New Zealand.

Henry Thompson on his motorcycle.

When the Queen of England made a state visit to New Zealand, Henry, with his mind fully on his ministry failed to give attention to this special event. On the day Her Majesty, the Queen, arrived by ocean liner, Henry started to his territory, mounted on his multicolored motorcycle. After all, he was on the King's business! When he reached the large boulevard that led to the wharf where the royal ship was anchored, he found the boulevard crowded with people lining each side, waiting for a glimpse of the Queen. Henry pushed his motorcycle through the friendly crowd, and people said, "Henry, it's clear. She hasn't started yet."

As Henry started down the wide boulevard, people began clapping their hands and calling, "There goes ol' Henry!"

Next morning's newspaper pictured Henry Thompson on his way to his territory, riding his motorcycle down the famous boulevard lined with spectators. The article was entitled "The Queen's Outrider."

Some Day I Will Meet You in Heaven – Home!

Emma Zell was a very grateful lady. In a letter to the conference office she wrote:

> These two men were such sincere Christians. My husband was seriously ill. We did not buy at the time of their visit. When they left, one of them offered such a beautiful prayer for our welfare, our health. He asked God's blessing on us and on our home. I cannot express to you what that prayer meant to me.

> I wish I had taken their names. If ever there were two Christian men it was those two who knocked at my door. After prayer it seemed that I saw Jesus knocking at my door and that I had opened the door and let Jesus in.

> When the younger man left he handed me a pamphlet, 'Man's Need of Christ'. If you happen to know these men, tell them how much that beautiful prayer meant to me. God bless you. Some day I will meet you in heaven – Home![157]

This story provides a view of persons waiting for a Christian visit, and gives a glimpse into the ministry of literature evangelists. They pray with and for the people whether or not a sale is made. Day after day literature evangelists touch hearts for God in a direct personal manner. *"To deal with human minds is the greatest work ever given to man."*[158] Jesus said, *"I counsel Thee to buy of Me. . . "*[159]

Promoted to Bell Ringer

Early in the author's Adventist church journey, annual

[157]Letter from Emma Zell, Madison, Iowa, February 22, 1977.
[158]Gospel Workers, p. 122, C.M., p. 74.
[159]Revelation 3:18.

camp meetings were part of our family life. It was there
that I first learned about literature evangelism. Stories by
colporteurs told in the big tent were exciting. I wondered
if some day I might have a part in that experience. For
forty years I did share with literature evangelists, Adventist
Book Center and publishing house personnel as I served
as publishing director in two local conferences, four union
conferences, three divisions, and the General Conference.
My life's mission exceeded my dreams.

When we attended camp meetings, my mother
arranged for my sister, Pauline, my brother, Chester, and
me to do various chores on the campground to help pay
expenses. I washed dishes, slept in a cold mattress tent, and
worked on the grounds. As I grew older, time came when
I was assigned official bell ringer for the campground. I
accepted this assignment with one concern – the rising bell.
What if I should oversleep? That dreaded day came! Greatly
concerned over my failure, I hastily ran out and vigorously
rang the rising bell. The sleeping saints were suddenly fully
awake.

Back in my tent I was startled when I heard voices
through canvas walls! "John, there is something wrong with
our clock!" I rubbed my eyes and again looked at my clock,
only to discover that I had unintentionally arranged for an
extra hour of camp meeting for that great encampment of
trusting souls. Soon guests arrived with the correct time and
some kindly counsel.

Language Discovery

To truly understand a people, one must learn their
language. While studying the Indonesian (Malay) language,
the writer discovered the importance of choosing and using
words correctly. Some words sound much alike but have
very different meanings.

I invited Dr. Donald Holm, a new missionary, to accompany me to visit Ennie, a native girl who was ill. I suggested that this could be his first opportunity to view native life and render medical service. Two Malay words "susa" (trouble) and "susu" (milk) can be confused. As we entered Ennie's little dwelling I said, "Ennie, sorry you are having so much "susu"! She carefully corrected me and the good doctor was unaware of my mistake.

Clothesline Information

Before electric and gas clothes dryers, people hung their laundry to dry in the sun The alert literature evangelist approaching the home of a prospective customer studies the house and its surroundings. Included in this study are garments hanging on the clothesline. This was especially so in wintertime in the northern lands where people wore long winter underwear. Strung out across the line were father's and mother's large underwear, also children's in varied sizes. This provided the bookman with a head count and approximate ages of children before he knocked on the door.

In Colorado at the foot of Pike's Peak where the author grew up water pipes were buried six feet below surface to prevent freezing. At our home there was no electric washer or dryer. I helped my mother hang out long underwear, which quickly froze on the line. Drying in the cold air, the arms and legs would fill with air and freeze, giving the appearance of headless figures suspended horizontally on a long wire whipped by a strong, icy wind.

For advance information today the literature evangelist will count the number and class of automobiles, boats, and ATVs surrounding a residence.

Changing Times

We live in a rapidly changing world. At one time people lived at the end of a dirt road, chopped and carried firewood or buckets of coal for heating, drew water from a well, cistern or nearby stream, and a man's word was his bond.

E-mails are now replacing letters; TV has replaced conversation. But there will never be a true replacement for the gospel in printed form.

In 1915 many vehicles for transportation were horses kept in livery stables. The author in his lifetime has seen the development of major highways, of early radio, TV, and travel by jet aircraft. I personally witnessed the harsh ending of colonialism. No longer do we hear of French Indo-China, Dutch East Indies or British Malaya. They have receded into history.

The author's uncle lived in a time of change. His second automobile came with a self-starter. Having always successfully cranked his first car to start it, there was no question in his mind but that a self-starter represented trouble. Therefore he removed the self-starter and continued cranking!

"Credit: Man's Confidence in Man."

A familiar story tells about the clerk at the check-out counter handing little Johnny a lollypop, and mother said, "What do you say to the kind lady?" Little Johnny quickly replied, "Charge it."

Wise or unwise, millions of individuals living in western hard currency nations float on a sea of credit. For

a literature evangelist family man to succeed economically,
he must offer his books on a monthly payment schedule.
Although large cash sales are not uncommon, provision for
credit sales is necessary. Whether we like it or not, we live
and work in our present real world.

A Dream Becomes Reality – A Church and a Church School

Upon retirement the author's parents moved from
Colorado to Arkansas. There my mother continued her
non-stop missionary ministry of giving two to three Bible
studies each week to neighbors and newfound friends. The
result of her self-appointed labors was 60 to 70 baptisms.
It began 90 years ago when a layman who had become a
literature evangelist visited my mother's uncle and sold him
a copy of *The Great Controversy*. The message of *The Great
Controversy* radiated through my mother's life until her
death.

The Southwestern Union Record reported my
mother's missionary work in Pocahontas, Arkansas:

The C. L. Wickwire family moved into
this community, the first Seventh-day Adventists.
Through Sister Wickwire's ceaseless efforts the
church company grew, and a representative building
was erected. Later the first Pocahontas church school
was established with eight students attending.[160]

My mother's devotion to the church influenced my
life. Her philosophy is well stated by Tolstoy, the famous
Russian philosopher: *"The main purpose of life is to serve
humanity."*

My mother died while I was serving the church in

---

[160] Information taken from Southwestern Union Record, 1954.

the Far Eastern Division. I was visiting in Korea at the time. Due to war it was not possible for me to return to the States for my mother's funeral. I was told that many businessmen of the city were present. Annually they had responded to her Ingathering appeals. Each year she presented to the church $400.00 to $500.00 for Ingathering.

This dedication to God and His church is repeated thousands of times, the result of the ministry of just one literature evangelist.

You Can't Take It, and Neither Can I

Among my mother's converts was the wife of the sheriff of Pocahontas, Arkansas. When newly married the couple began as sharecroppers on rich river-bottom land. During planting and harvest time they worked long days, from before daybreak into the twilight hours. He worked his mules as hard as he worked himself. To save time for a quick start in the morning, he left the heavy harness on his mules during the short nights.

He saved his hard-earned money, soon owned land, and was no longer a sharecropper. Next, he began buying city rental properties until he owned several. He became well known and was elected sheriff.

Retired when I met him, his hands and body gave evidence of hard work. When he became sick and died, many attended his funeral. As his body was being lowered into the earth, his wife, watching the lowering casket, seemed overcome with the memory of a harsh life of disciplined economic conquest and cried aloud, "Money, money, money! You can't take it with you, and neither can I!"

Chapter 14 - The Gift of a Simple Man

Elder Stan Patterson, Ministerial Director of the Georgia-Cumberland Conference, tells how his family became Christians and then Seventh-day Adventists:

He was a simple man and drove a ten year old, faded green 1949 Dodge sedan.[161] I suppose it could be said that we were simple people – four brothers, no sisters, and a Dad and Mom that worked too hard and had too little.

The rented farm home faced a dusty road that often saw the shadow of a car but once a day when Mr. Chance, the postman, faithfully brought the mail and roared off in a cloud of dust, unless it was raining, in which case he saved the mail until the next day because the dust changed to mud, and ceased to be a road other than in name.

The barn sat about 250 yards northeast of the house. There about three dozen Holsteins and a few mixed breed milk cows were milked twice a day, thus providing means to help support the daily needs of the family of six. The north side of the barn was home to a herd of hogs, who waded through the naked corncobs that lay everywhere as reminders of past meals.

It was to this old red barn amid the activity of afternoon chores that the simple man came. Somehow he had parked the old green Dodge and had gotten past the brown dog that guarded the entrance to the lives of these six people. The man's face bore lines that betrayed the accumulation of years, and his hands were gnarled and marked with the labor of those same years. His left hand grasped a scuffed brown leather satchel that promised to reveal the reason for his visit. His right hand greeted each of us.

---

[161] Story furnished by Elder Stanley Patterson, Ministerial Director for GA-Cumberland Conference of Seventh-day Adventists.

A professional salesman he was not. He was not dressed as such, and he didn't act like one, which was to his advantage, because those in the barn didn't trust professional salesman much and usually didn't have the wherewithal to buy their wares anyway. John, as his introduction revealed, was too unassuming to be a real salesman. He actually looked more like a farmer, and not out of place standing next to the bales of straw that leaned against the rough oak divider.

With the satchel resting on a bale of straw he reached into its cavity and drew out a book. The exposed edges were printed in a marbled pattern popular in those days. Its thickness set it apart as unique. Other than the occasional Zane Grey or Edgar Rice Boroughs novel checked out from the country bookmobile that made its monthly rounds, no other books were found in our humble setting and definitely none so thick. The proverbial "Family Bible" might have been thicker, but this family did not possess a Bible. The thick book with the marbled edges didn't seem to stand a chance of changing hands.

Try as he gently might, the simple man could not make a sale. He explained that it was a Christian book, *Bible Readings for the Home Circle*. He turned the marble edged pages and revealed its contents of questions and references to the four brothers, who had already lost interest and a Dad who was anxious to finish with the equally impatient cows.

The simple man's visit ended with a concession. He laid the book on the bale of straw. As he turned to go he concluded by saying, "I'll be back in a week. If you want the book you may pay me then, if not, I'll pick it up." With that he made his way past the feed wagon, out the door and up the hill to his old Dodge, unaware that he had changed forever the lives of these six people and many scores of others.

Dad rolled a cigarette of Prince Albert tobacco and

carried the book into the house, where he laid it on the wide arm of the chair we knew as his. Supper came and went with little notice given as he followed his usual routine and sat down in his chair. Actually, a break in routine went mostly unnoticed as he pulled the chain on the pedestal lamp over his shoulder and opened the book with the marble edges. Few were aware of Dad's difficulty with reading. He never read aloud and had spent little time reading silently. Most of his time was spent working and most of the rest was spent sleeping so he could get up and work again.

The change in routine became noticeable as he spent more and more time with the book. Odd that a book of questions could prove so fascinating. The four brothers didn't understand the fascination and Mom didn't seem to have a clue either, except that Dad seemed to spend a little less time working, and gave up some of his sleep.

The days passed and once again the 1949 Dodge rumbled ahead of a cloud of dust and came to a stop at our house. Old John mounted the steps of the porch and was met at the door by Dad with the book in his extended hand. "I'd be interested in this book (the thick one with the marbled edges) but it seems I'd need a Bible for it to make much sense, and I don't own one."

"I'm trying to decide, Madame, whether you qualify to be one of the privileged few to whom I may show our product."

With that comment the scuffed leather satchel once again came open, not to replace the book held out by Dad but rather to reveal a box containing a leather bound Bible which had gold embossed edges. "I sell Bibles," said John, and the deal was done. A simple man who wasn't much of a salesman had sold a Christian book and a Bible to a man who wasn't a Christian.

Dad's new routine became predictable. Work, eat, study the marble edged book with the Bible at his side, and then sleep. He wasn't much for talk before he bought the book, and became less so afterwards. Weeks passed into months, and he became a Christian without a church. Uncle John, as he preferred to be called, went to a church about fifty miles distant. Dad began attending the local Southern Baptist church that gladly welcomed him and Mom and the four brothers. Not only did the Bible become a part of daily life, but now Sundays and weekday revival meetings became the pattern of life.

A baptism marked a high point of this family's spiritual transition. Dad, Mom and two of the brothers were baptized in the clear, cool waters of a tank built into the floor of the platform in the church, as the congregation sang "Just As I Am" and "I Surrender All."

Dad who would never have read aloud only a few months before was now asked to teach a Sunday school class. There were no prepared materials. The thick book with the marble edges became the foundation for lessons that were taught each Sunday morning. Having never been exposed to Christianity as a child, Dad's naiveté regarding sectarian attitudes among Christians became very evident. What he found in his marble edged book and his new Bible is what he taught. For all its goodness and its love this little Southern Baptist Church wasn't ready to discuss the seventh day Sabbath.

The preacher, short and fiery as he was, came to the house only to find Dad plowing corn in some far field. Mom spoke to him through the screen door, and the brothers stood in the shadows of the room listening. In concluding his counsel the preacher pointed to the boys and said, "If your husband persists with this idea of Sabbath it could cause those boys to burn in the fires of hell!" Much to the discomfort of the eavesdroppers, he sounded as if he meant it.

Dad lacked a lot of things, but courage wasn't one of them. Something within drove him to stay with the Bible as he read it. He and Mom left the little Baptist church and once again became Christians without a church home. Uncle John stopped by occasionally and on one visit suggested that Dad consider taking advantage of the radio as a partial replacement for the church he had lost. Old John introduced Dad to a program that not only had preaching and music, but also would send him Bible lessons that he could follow by mail. It wasn't long until "Life Up the Trumpet" became as familiar as "Just As I Am." A man with the strange name of H.M.S. was the preacher and the Kings Herald Quartet became the choir. Dad bought an old reel-to-reel tape player and began ordering tapes of sermons and music that played for hours on end.

Thinking back it is amazing how patient Old Uncle John was. He was a simple man who had accepted the call to become a fisher of men. He had cast out the bait, got Dad to nibble, waited patiently for him to take it for real, and was now ready to set the hook – he offered to pick Dad up and take him to church. Dad was the second point in a triangular route that Uncle John had to travel in order to get to church. Thirty miles to pick up Dad, fifty miles to church, and a repeat of that route to get home. John was now reeling him in.

On Tuesday night prior to Dad's first trip to this church God gave him a dream. It wasn't earthshaking as dreams go, but it seemed odd to dream of a woman standing in the pulpit teaching from the Bible. Women weren't allowed to teach from the pulpit in the Southern Baptist Church. Little thought was given to the dream before leaving with Uncle John on Saturday morning to go to church. That, by the way, was the Sabbath Dad had discovered in the Bible and the book with the marble edges. It was startling to Dad to walk into the church a few minutes before 10:00 a.m. and come face to face with the woman he had seen in his dream as she taught the Sabbath School lesson.

Do We Have to Sell the Hogs?

Dad made the decision to become a Seventh-day Adventist in 1959. Mom struggled with the idea of such a radical change. "Isn't it enough to be the only people in the county to go to church on Saturday? Do we have to sell the hogs?"

Mom's love for Dad and the undeniably clear counsel from the Bible led to both of them being rebaptized as Seventh-day Adventist Christians. Later the fifth and last brother was born into the Seventh-day Adventist home, followed six years later by a sister. Today three of the six children serve in various denominational leadership positions. Dad and Mom continue to serve the church they joined nearly forty years ago. A family changed forever by the faithfulness of a simple man in a faded 1949 Dodge sedan.

One day Jesus will call from the grave those who have been awaiting the command, "Arise and sing ye who dwell in the dust!" and that simple man we knew as Uncle John will come forth singing. If it is true that the stars in our crowns of glory will represent the souls we have helped deliver from the prison house of death, then Uncle John's will be heavy indeed.

I know you can't hear me, but thanks Uncle John.

Chapter 15 – Reaping

Large Evangelistic Reaping Meetings

As church members in western nations we thrill with reports of large evangelistic crusade reaping meetings in so-called developing countries. How can these be? In a large part the answer is that for more than a century, hundreds and then thousands of literature evangelists have been sowing gospel seed at home and abroad. God promised the harvest. *"In the morning sow thy seed, and in the evening withhold not thine hand."*[162] The effort of preparing the soil and planting the seed is accomplished by combined human and divine effort. With the Lord of the Harvest watching over the gospel seed, the harvest is certain.

How Beautiful Upon the Mountains

While attending a large literature evangelist institute in the Philippine Islands in 1977 the writer watched a brave, sturdy, barefoot young literature evangelist go forward to tell of his ministry in a dangerous mountain village. Scars revealed that he had been beaten, yet with him were three young trophies from that village. They stayed close by his side; he had risked his life for them, they loved him. During that institute the three were baptized. This bookman's rugged, bare feet told the story of Isaiah 52:7: *"How beautiful upon the mountains are the feet of him that bringeth good tidings, that publisheth peace, that bringeth good tidings of good . . . "*

---

[162]Ecclesiastes 11:6.

Majority of Soul-Winning Contacts
-- "We Never Hesitate to Invest" --

The Philippine unions operate special literature evangelist training centers. One Philippine union president said, "We never hesitate to invest money in our publishing work, for it is from this family-to-family ministry by these evangelistic workers that we realize the majority of our soul-winning contacts." At one time the Central Luzon field alone employed more than twenty-five publishing leaders!

Literature Evangelists of the Philippines, As Far as the Eye Can See.

What It Did For a Nation

In the year 1905, a young man, R. A. Caldwell, sitting in the North Fitzroy church in Melbourne, Australia, was impressed with the need for someone to go to the Philippines. He volunteered. He was the first Seventh-day Adventist to work in this 7,000-island empire. At that time there were no Seventh-day Adventists in the Philippines, nor was there any church organization. Today the author is told that there are 800,000 Seventh-day Adventist church members, and 8,000 literature evangelists.

When Caldwell boarded ship to return permanently to his homeland, he said of the books he had placed in the homes of the people of the Philippines, "They are the leaven that will move the mass." How true his predictions.

While the author was serving as director of the church's world publishing literature ministry he was privileged in 1977 to attend the largest single convention of house-to-house evangelistic church workers ever held by Seventh-day Adventists, and this was in the Philippines. At that time there were 3,000 Philippine literature evangelists. Of that number 2,500 had qualified to attend this great spiritual convocation held in the mountain city of Baguio.

Philippine Literature Evangelists Meet in Baguio, 1977.

In the midst of the pageantry stories revealed soul-winning conquests. I realized anew the impact literature evangelism had made on an entire nation and that reaping time was at hand.

National Council of Philippine Publishing Department Leaders, 1978.

The Answer is Profound

Throughout the world church members leave secular employment to become literature evangelists, aware that one who "leaves his nets" to follow the Lord will encounter trials. They read the signs of the times and truly believe that Jesus is coming , and that it is possible to hasten that great event.

Dealing With Minds

In our fast moving society literature evangelists are taught how to arrest the attention of busy minds long enough to plant gospel seed. Many minds are like dry, parched ground. When given a short cloudburst of information, most of it runs off. However, each time a gospel sale is consummated serious mind engagement has occurred. Strangers detect the soul-winning heartbeat of the visitor who calls at their door.

In response to his prayers the literature evangelist feels assured that angels precede him on his mission and that the Holy Spirit assists his efforts. Wise is the administrator who deals gently with the divine ministry of literature evangelists.

When Jesus met the Samaritan woman who had come to draw water from Jacob's well, He asked a favor instead of granting one. He did not speak of a camel caravan passing in the distance. He spoke of water, the object of her obvious interest. After He received a drink of water from Jacob's well, He directed her attention to "Living Water." Her response, "*Sir, give me this water that I thirst not. . .*"[163] Day by day, family by family, literature evangelists follow the Master's evangelistic technique. The secret is "see the people" one by one. People thirst for living water.

[163] John 4:15

So Long Coming. Why?

After a well-presented gospel sales appeal these questions are common:
"Is this something new?"

"Why haven't I heard this before?"

"I wish I had had this when my children were growing up."

"Goodnight, I Will See You in the Morning"

While the author was serving the publishing ministry of the Orient he was appointed as Publishing Director of the Far Eastern Division in 1950. World War II weapons were rusting on the beaches. On my first official visit to the Philippine Islands Dr. Andrew Nelson invited me to speak to Japanese prisoners of war, officers being held in the Abilibid Prison near the city of Manila.

Seated on the cement floor were seventy men dressed in orange prison suits, heads shaved, awaiting death. They had been condemned to die for wartime atrocities, Dr. Andrew Nelson, President of the Japan Union, fluent in the Japanese language, had conducted Bible studies inside those prison walls. Seventeen of these men of war had accepted the message of the three angels.

For that unusual occasion I chose as my subject, "The Certainty of our Faith," my remarks intended primarily for the seventeen newly committed Christians in the audience. The future of each man was understandably foreboding. Some of their fellows had preceded them to the gallows.

One week later I was told that two of the men in that

audience had been taken to the gallows, one a converted
Christian, the other true to his Shinto beliefs. The Shinto
believer struggled down the long hallway to the gallows.
The Christian convert walked as bravely as possible toward
the gallows accompanied by Dr. Andrew Nelson. With hope
beyond this life he faced death with faith and trust.

When the two men sharing faith in Christ reached a
certain point in the long hallway, a guard touched Dr. Nelson
on the shoulder and said, "Sir, you are not permitted beyond
this point." At that moment the condemned military officer,
now a soldier of Jesus Christ, extended his hand to Dr.
Nelson and said, "Goodnight, I will see you in the morning."
There is power, unimaginable power, in the gospel of Jesus
Christ.

Eternal Subscription

A Mohammedan subscriber to the Indonesian version
of *Signs of the Times*, *Pertandan Zamin* living in Borneo
(now Kalimantan), wrote complaining about the journal.

The writer replied thanking him for his concern,
and mentioned that Seventh-day Adventists have much
in common with Moslems, especially in the areas of diet
(no pork) and temperance (no alcohol or tobacco). He
responded, expressing appreciation for my explanation and
said that he wanted an "eternal subscription." In Indonesia,
with the largest Moslem population on earth, hogs are found
only in Christian sections of the nation.

Publishing Ministry in Hungary

In 1950 when there were 120 literature evangelists in
Hungary, the government closed down all evangelistic work.

Toward the end of 1988 permission was again granted for Seventh-day Adventist literature to be sold in Hungary. Newspapers told about the sale of books by Seventh-day Adventists. One clipping said, "These people are people of conviction. They tell you that they have the truth." This commends their courage and conviction.

Poland

Poland, a nation which had too often served as a corridor for marching armies, had reopened its doors for person-to-person evangelism after a seventeen year restrictive ban. Literature evangelists need no longer fear nor endure imprisonment. When the author first visited Poland in 1966 the ban had just been removed. It was an honor to conduct a gospel sales institute, marking renewed freedom for literature evangelists. Books and magazines were packaged according to requests by respective literature evangelists, and placed on the floor surrounding the pulpit in the Warsaw Seventh-day Adventist Church. It was a small mountain of literature ready for distribution. At this solemn, never-to-be-forgotten occasion special prayer was offered, petitioning God to bless the new beginning

Government publishers had censored and printed our books and journals, including *The Great Controversy*. One government censor, after reading the message contained in the book *The Great Controversy*, became a Seventh-day Adventist.

The Porcelain Arrived Unbroken

While conducting literature evangelist institutes in Poland in 1967, the author was privileged to meet Adventist pastors visiting from the USSR. Bibles were forbidden in

Russia at that time, and there was a longing for the Holy
Scriptures.

Seventh-day Adventist believers in Russia secretly
translated and produced Sabbath School lessons and some
Spirit of Prophecy books, by means of typewriters and
multiple carbon copies. Before leaving London for Warsaw
I had been asked to take a set of Sabbath School lessons for
use in the USSR. I also took Volume I of the ten volume *The
Bible Story* set, and a Bible in the Russian language.

For three days during my visit I traveled with these
Russian church leaders visiting various church groups. When
one of these ministers was preparing to return to the USSR
by train, I visited him in his hotel room. There I learned
that he had created a false bottom in his suitcase in order
to conceal the Sabbath School lessons and *The Bible Story*
book. I was surprised to notice the complete cover of the
new Russian Bible lying on a table in his room, so I asked
what had happened to the Bible.

My friend unbuttoned his coat. Hidden under his
shirt, secured by his belt, was the Russian Bible, separated
into three parts, strapped to his body. He would wear the
Bible back to his country.

We told him good-bye at the Warsaw train station. A
few hours later the following cable message was received:
The Porcelain Arrived Unbroken! We thanked the Lord!

In Fifty Years, 104 Souls by One Literature Evangelist

Rudi Henning, former Associate General Conference
Publishing Director, in telling of publishing progress in

Austria, spoke of a lady literature evangelist who had been working for fifty years. She was especially honored at the Literature Evangelist Institute in Austria. With great joy she reported that through her service 104 persons had been baptized. Definitely, those who win souls are wise [Proverbs 11:30].

Germany

It was Catholic Priest Martin Luther of Germany who with the power of the printing press, shook the foundation of his church and brought about the Reformation.

In more recent times L.R. Conradi wrote tracts and established the colporteur work in Germany. Also Gerhard Perk, an early Russian convert, who fled Russia to Germany to escape persecution, and Emil Frauchiger, a Swiss believer, came to Germany to sell *Das Leben Jesu*, (The Life of Christ).[164]

The author recalls meeting some of Germany's large army of "Book Evangelists," as their colporteurs are called. They are supported by union and local conference administrations, and the strong Hamburg Publishing House.

A Thousand Shall Fall

The thrilling story of Franz Hasel, a Seventh-day Adventist literature evangelist, who dared to practice his faith in Hitler's army, is recorded in the book, *A Thousand Shall Fall,* written by his daughter, Susi Hasel Mundy. It tells of the Pioneers, Hitler's elite troops to which Hasel had been assigned, being transferred to Poland in 1940. It was in Poland that Hasel's expertise in typing, office work, and

[164] Seventh-day Adventist Encyclopedia, p. 509.

organizational skills, acquired during years of doing literature evangelist and publishing work helped him receive a new assignment as Obergefreiter, first company clerk. With this assignment came privileges, but the privilege he appreciated the most was that he could arrange his work schedule in such a way that he always had Sabbath off.[165]

Final Report – Netherlands

J. Lijkendijk, Director, Publishing Department, Netherlands Union Conference in 1969, reported on the death of veteran literature evangelist, Brother J. van Lakerveld. This brother had often said he wanted to keep working until four days before his burial. His last day of work was five days before he was laid to rest.

Brother van Lakerveld's last weekly literature evangelist report, which he had completed the afternoon he became ill, was taken to the post box that afternoon. When he went to his rest the following evening, he had finished the task his Master had given him to do.

Soon, very soon, the trumpet will sound. Brother van Lakeraveld, who quietly went to sleep at nearly eighty-two years of age, after spending forty years telling the story of salvation with the printed page, will rise in the vigor of youth to meet many who will say, "It was you who invited me here."

Spreading the Gospel in South America

General Conference Associate Publishing Director, Rudi Henning visited Brazil in 1979. He reported almost 3,000 regular and student literature evangelists working in Brazil at that time, and the presses in the Brazil Publishing

---

[165] Susi Mundy and Maylan Schurch, A Thousand Shall Fall, p. 36.

House running full capacity, two shifts a day to produce the
needed literature. They were still unable to meet the growing
demand for literature.

Literature Evangelists of Brazil

Brazil's strong publishing ministry is revealed in the
life of one of its champion literature evangelists, Antonio
Zuza. Since starting in the literature ministry a number
of years ago he has sold over 80,000 copies of *The Great
Controversy.*

"Saturnino Mendes de Oliveira, one of the early
colporteur directors in Brazil, was associated with colporteur
work for 41 consecutive years before retiring. During that
time he is reported to have visited or worked in more than
820 cities and villages in Brazil."[166] Little wonder Brazil
maintains one of the church's largest literature evangelist
programs.

Administrative belief in and support of the soul
winning power of literature evangelism makes the Brazil
Publishing House a beacon of light and provides economic
strength to the church in Brazil.

[166] Seventh-day Adventist Encyclopedia, p. 189.

Planting Adventism in Argentina More Than a Century Ago

"Look Pedro! Look, Cecilia! I have just received a magazine from our old hometown of Torre Pellice in Italy. It has strange things to say." Daniel Rostan waved the paper as he entered the little general merchandise store in Las Garzas, northern Argentina.[167]

Daniel had come to share the news with his friends the Peverinis. Cecilia was a Waldensian like himself, and Pedro was practically an atheist. They had all emigrated from Italy a decade before. Now in the 1880s were trying to make a living on the Argentine frontier.

"Sit down, Daniel. Tell us all about it. What's so exciting?" responded Pedro as he offered the older man a chair.

Literature Evangelists of Paraguay.

"Here it tells about a religious group called Seventh-day Adventists who predict the end of the world," said Daniel. "The author declares that they need not print their magazine *Les Signes des Temps* (Signs of the Times) on such good paper stock if the world is going to burn up soon."

Ceclia listened intently. Although Pedro was not religious, she loved the Bible and read it to her children every day. She had some questions in her mind about Bible doctrine. "I would like to see the magazine your paper mentions, Daniel," she suggested. "It might solve some problems I have discovered in my Bible reading."

---

[167] Story by Robert Wearner, *Adventist Review*, November 21, 1985.

"Why don't you write to your brother in Torre Pellice?" Pedro offered. "He might be able to find the magazine. I would like to study the prophecies of the end of the world myself."

A letter was soon on its way. Cecilia's brother sent a subscription for *Les Signes des Temps* to the Peverinis, who were happy to share their copies with the Rostans.

Both families became interested in Bible prophecies. Again Daniel came to visit the Peverinis. "What do you think about those articles in the magazine teaching that Saturday is the right day to keep?" he questioned.

"It's right there in the Ten Commandments: 'Remember the Sabbath day, to keep it holy.' Don't forget, Jesus kept only the seventh day. It's clear enough to me," declared Cecilia. "I discovered this in my own Bible sometime ago."

In 1885, after much study and prayer, the two families decided to observe the Bible Sabbath, thinking they were the only Christian Sabbath keepers in South America.

Eight years slipped by. One day in 1893 a tall young foreigner entered Peverini's store and canvassed them for a book called *The Great Controversy*. They soon discovered he was a Seventh-day Adventist, the first they had ever seen. Needless to say, the Peverinis and the Rostans received the new colporteur with open arms. Eagerly they purchased *The Great Controversy* and *Patriarchs and Prophets* in French. Lionel Brooking, the young colporteur, was greatly encouraged by his visit to the Peverinis and Rostans. He instructed them in the Adventist way of life.

In 1896 a Seventh-day Adventist minister, Jean Vuilleumier, from Switzerland, came to northern Argentina.

Pedro and Cecilia Peverini and the Rostan family were
baptized after Pastor Vuilleumier studied with them. In 1897
a church was organized in Las Garzas.

Two years later Pastor Frank Westphal, a pioneer
missionary, came to Las Garzas to hold a short camp meeting
in a tent pitched in the Peverinis' yard. People came by
wagon or on horseback from as far as 50 miles. With
Pastor Westphal was N. Z. Town, a colporteur leader. Town
reported 40 Sabbath keepers in the area at that time. He
prepared six young men who had volunteered to become
colporteurs (literature evangelists).

When Adventists of Entre Rios were starting a school,
Pedro, a builder, traveled to the new college site and offered
his services free of charge.

Son Daniel Peverini and his wife Amalia Mazza
sent all their nine children to River Plate College, the
school Pedro had helped build. Today one of Daniel's
grandsons, Milton, serves as director-speaker for La Voz de
la Esperanza (Voice of Hope), our Spanish broadcast heard
on three continents. His twin brother, Tulio, edits the Pacific
Press Spanish publications. The Daniel Rostan family also
produced several workers for the church.

Sowing Gospel Seed in Chile
What Inspired Fred and Tom?

Thousands of Chilean Adventists, from the hot desert
of the north to the frozen, barren south, thank God for Fred
Bishop and Tom Davis.[168] Who were these brave men? What
inspired them in 1894 to do colporteur work in Chile?

F. L. Mead, an Adventist publishing department
leader, found Fredrick Bishop at Healdsburg College (now

[168] Story by Robert Wearner, Adventist Review, July 31, 1986.

Pacific Union College). "Fred," he said, "You have been a successful colporteur here in California. Why don't you go to Chile to pioneer the work of God in that country?"

"I'll go anywhere the Lord calls me," Fred responded, "but I would like a little time to pray about it." Fred had sold books all summer and was about to enroll for his third year at Healdsburg College. Should he continue his studies or take the message of a soon-coming Saviour to a dark corner of South America?

By Sunday morning Fred had made up his mind. He had already deposited money at the school with the idea of studying during the fall term, but now he accepted the colporteur leader's suggestion to do self-supporting work in Chile. The college president refunded his deposit.

In the meantime F. L. Mead found another volunteer for mission service, Thomas H. Davis, who consented to accompany Fred. That September the two young men booked passage on a steamship bound for Valparaiso, Chile. To save money, they reserved the cheapest cabin. The rest of their funds they invested in books to sell and blankets to keep themselves warm, leaving only $2.50 by the time they embarked. With faith in their hearts, and a prayer on their lips they bade farewell to their loved ones and sailed out of the Golden Gate.

"Well, Fred, here we are! This coastal area[169] looks desolate," observed Tom, as their ship steamed into the harbor of Valparaiso on December 8, 1894. Shortly after landing, the new colporteurs met Clair Nowlen, who had spent two years selling books in Argentina and the Falkland Islands. Nowlen soon returned to Argentina, leaving his stock of books with Fred and Tom.

---

[169] The coast line of Chile extends 2,650 miles.

I'll Go South, You Go North

After selling a few books in the Valparaiso area, Tom and Fred separated. Davis took a train south to the agricultural area of Victoria where he sold 100 large books over a six month period. Fred Bishop boarded a ship that took him 900 miles to the north, where he landed at Iquique. In this desert area he succeeded in selling copies of the Spanish *Patriarchs and Prophets*.

Almost Evicted – Wife to the Rescue

After a number of months the two young men met again and decided to work in the national capital, Santiago, a city of 250,000 at that time. They boarded with a Baptist minister from Spain, Enrique Balada. When Balada discovered they were Sabbath keepers he set about to show them the "error" of their doctrine. After several nights of Bible study the Baptist minister saw that he was getting nowhere with the young men. Incensed at his tenants, he complained to his wife, "What do these young fellows think they are doing – trying to teach me, a preacher?"

"And what do they teach that is wrong?" she quietly asked.

"They say we should keep the seventh day."

"They are quite right, too," she countered. "That's the only day the Bible teaches us to observe, and I intend to keep it!"

The minister was shocked, but in time he, too, was persuaded. Later he became a Seventh-day Adventist minister, serving faithfully for many years.

Overheard Talking While Walking

In the meantime Tom and Fred were trying to find ways to improve their Spanish. "What do you think of this method?" suggested Fred. "You read a verse from your English Bible, and I'll read the same text from my Spanish version."

They chose the book of Psalms, which they read to each other as they walked along Alameda Avenue, one of the principal streets of the city. As they were reading Psalm 103 they noticed a young man watching them intently. Finally he approached and introduced himself as Victor Thomann, a Swiss wood-carver. He told the two colporteurs of his desire to study the Bible.

Tom and Fred invited Victor to their lodgings where they studied with him by pointing to texts in the Spanish Bible. Victor told them that sometime before he dreamed of seeing two young men walking along Alameda Avenue reading Psalm 103, the very scripture the colporteurs were studying when he approached. Convinced that God had led him to these young men, he quickly accepted their message.

Davis and Bishop continued selling books up and down the country of Chile for several years. Thomas Davis and his first wife became the first Adventist missionaries to South America to die in their field of labor. Frederick Bishop continued to colporteur until 1921, when he and his wife retired to a farm until his death in 1929. A number of his descendants became workers in the church, including several with the surname Vyhmeister.

In 1894 two young men chose to dedicate their lives to sowing the gospel seed in Chile. After nine decades an abundant harvest of souls – 50,000 in 200 churches – shows that they did not labor in vain.

Thailand

Thailand is a land of ornate temples, four hundred in number. It is also a land of elephants, tigers, oxcarts, and river traffic. "Most young men become monks for short periods, usually three months. They wear yellow robes and beg for their food. Their yellow raiment singles them out as worthy of alms."[170]

The author's first visit to Thailand, earlier known as Siam, was by train in 1949. World War II had recently ended. The locomotive pushed a railway flat car loaded with sand weighted to detonate explosive land mines enroute. It was at

Thailand Literature Evangelists - 1950

night, and we were traveling in a crude sleeper railroad car. Armed British soldiers were above, before, and behind me. Placed along the wall of my sleeper section were pillows to slow any bullets which might be encountered in the event of an ambush. The railway line to Bangkok was interrupted by damaged or missing bridges. Intervals of the journey were undertaken by bus.

Annually the writer visited each mission territory, conducting full-scale gospel sales training classes. On one occasion I actually canvassed in the town of Haad Jai (Thailand) with the help of a translator.

Grateful for Colporteurs

In 1951 Thailand Mission President, Pastor Wayne A. Martin wrote of how grateful he was for the work of

[170] TWA Vacation Guide and World Atlas, p. 204.

the colporteurs in Thailand. He said that colporteurs were taking the message to remote parts of the country, where the few regular pastors would not have time or opportunity to go. The efforts of the pastor are thus multiplied, as he cultivates and harvests the seed sown by colporteurs. Pastor Martin felt that Jesus might well say, "Pray ye therefore the Lord of the harvest, that He will send forth more colporteurs into His harvest."[171]

Window on Life

Literature evangelists have access to a window on life, and are witnesses to a world in agony and confusion. Many working parents are too occupied to spend meaningful time with their God-given children. Merchants of misery have created an epidemic of child and teen abuse and isolation. When parents are awakened to the need to protect their children by the visit of a literature evangelist they reach for the hope found in our books.

Today considerable airline revenue results from divorced parents shuttling their children back and forth on national and international flights for parental visits, often unattended. Parents, anxious for the eternal good of their children, struggle with life's social and moral imbalance. The world cries for understanding and compassion.

Concerned Parents.

The Scriptures counsel parents to acquaint their children with heaven's code of conduct, the Ten Commandments, a guideline for living. Included in the books literature evangelists present is literature designed to assist parents in giving guidance to their children in their passage to adulthood. With tactful use of our publications, literature

[171]Letter from Wayne A. Martin, September 20, 1951.

evangelists direct parents to their Bibles.

On one occasion the author asked a mother to let him read to her the counsel found in Deuteronomy 6:6-9. *"And these words which I command you today shall be in your heart. You shall teach them diligently to your children, and shall talk of them when you sit in your house, when you walk by the way, when you lie down and when you rise up. You shall bind them as a sign on your hand, and they shall be as frontlets between your eyes. You shall write them on the doorposts of your house and on your gates. "*[172] After reading these verses from her Bible, I closed the Book. She said, "Oh, could you find those verses again. I want to mark them."

Cambodia's New Beginning

National & International Publishing Directors meet with
Cambodia's new Literature Evangelists
August 25-28, 2004 in Phnom Penh

John Brereton, Singapore (checkered shirt) and
Braam Oberholster, South Africa, center front.

[172] Deuteronomy 6:6-9, NKJV, The Inspirational Study Bible by Max Lucado.

Chapter 16 -
As Long As Probation Continues

This we must believe; literature evangelism was designed by God to continue until the angel sounds the final trumpet. The same voice, which said, *"Begin to Print,"* also said, *"As long as probation continues, there will be opportunity for the canvasser to work."* Where church leaders comprehend the evangelistic power inherent in the role of literature evangelists in world evangelism with evident and assured economic returns to the church treasury, there is opportunity for the canvasser to work. If human reasoning should be allowed to replace divine counsel, if faith should be lost, if honor should die, the mission of the church would be severely compromised, threatening its identity.

Since pioneer Joseph Bates began selling gospel tracts, hundreds of millions of personal home visits have been made by literature evangelists. The equivalent of unnumbered railroad train loads of books and journals have been placed in homes. Few have been destroyed. Still alive, they are found in attics, non-SDA church libraries, public libraries, and old bookstores. While people have trouble with their memories, the silent, persuasive messages in our books continually remind readers of God's love for man and produce a constant inflow of member families into the church.

Rooted Deeply

Converts from the ministry of the printed word are usually deeply rooted in the fundamental doctrines of the Seventh-day Adventist church. They are among the church's most supportive members. Personal spiritual contact with

human minds and hearts prepares the way for other church
ministries. The literature evangelist plows the field and
scatters the good seed over lands of earth. His labors are
fed and watered by the hand of God. "To do great things by
small means is the law of God."[173]

Harvest Acknowledges Seed-Sowing

The fact remains, "The press eclipses the orator."[174]
For one hundred fifty years Seventh-day Adventist editors
and authors have penned scriptural messages of hope.
Laymen as literature evangelists have carried these messages
into all the world. They have heeded the gospel commission,
*"And He said unto them, Go ye into all the world and preach
the gospel to every creature."*[175]

It is important to understand that laymen who become
literature evangelists could be doing less stressful work.
However, "When the Lord asks, 'Whom shall I send, and
who will go for Us?' the Divine Spirit puts it into human
hearts to respond."[176] Tens of thousands of Seventh-day
Adventist laymen have said, "Here am I; send me." For
more than one hundred years conferences of the church
as evangelistic supervisory centers and recipients of vast
economic returns, have supported and protected this response
to a Divine calling.

With wife and children dependent on income
from husband's literature evangelistic labors, brave men
struggle under pressure of economic uncertainties. At
such times I thank the Lord for leaders who understand
the soul-winning and economic returns from the ministry
of literature evangelists and without hesitation provide
reasonable subsidies for faithful service based on reasonable
requirements. Trusted "shepherds of the flock" will not be

[173] History of Reformation, Book 2, Chapter 1.
[174] Samuel C. Bartlett, Anniversary Addresses, Dartmouth College, p. 341.
[175] Mark 16:15.
[176] Testimonies, Vol. 6, p. 325, (1900), C.M., p. 43.

silent but will fulfill their responsibility by giving personal support and promotion to this ordained ministry. As long as General Conference and Division policy manuals identify the sacred role of literature evangelists, ensuring undistracted leadership, the impression will not be given that "They died as though they never lived and served."

Reflections – How Fortunate the Church

The soul-winning stories in this book tell of generous economic returns to the church, and provide a compelling reason why "the efficient colporteur, as well as the minister, should have sufficient remuneration for his services, if his work is faithfully done."[177] The result is tens of thousands of converts world wide, financially supporting this cause and influencing their children over succeeding generations to join them in this commitment.

Knowing the end from the beginning, the Lord through his servant said, *"As long as probation continues, there will be opportunity for the canvasser to work."*[178]

To the governing body of the church come both the responsibility and the privilege to ensure that *"The canvassing work should never languish. The agencies set in operation to do this work need always to be under the control of the Holy Spirit."*[179]

"As the end draws near, the work of God is to increase in full strength and purity and holiness."[180] "The presentation of the truth, in love and simplicity, from house to house is in harmony with the instruction that Christ gave to His disciples."[181] This time-proven ministry of literature

[177] Testimonies, Vol. 4, p. 390, (1880), C.M., p. 8.
[178] Testimonies, Vol. 6, p. 478, (1900), C.M., p. 11.
[179] Letter 82, (1889), C.M., p. 104.
[180] Review and Herald, September 17, 1903, C.M., p. 154.
[181] Testimonies, Vol. 9, p. 34, (1900), C.M., p. 83

evangelists requires conference administrative attention as does pastoral ministry.

Sobering Thoughts

While mortal men rule and mortal men die, the modern world flourishes as the child of doubt and skepticism. Yet purpose for life begins only when a person realizes how soon it ends. When the spiritual state of society in a community or in a nation appears hopeless, we must realize that nothing is impossible with God.

Freedoms

Possible future limitation of freedom of airways, satellite and radio commands attention and suggests need for continued encouragement and support of the ministry of Literature Evangelists.

As Long As Probation Continues

The first step in church publishing was taken by brave pioneers. The last step requires that same spirit **"as long as probation continues. . ."**

The foresight of early church leaders is evident in the role of literature evangelists in world evangelism. Their ministry is etched in the soil of every nation and every island and in the souls of their people. God ordained it so. May the church continue to invest in that which did so much to make it strong.